A THEORY OF
ECONOMIC HISTORY

A THEORY OF
ECONOMIC HISTORY

BY

JOHN HICKS

CLARENDON PRESS · OXFORD

1969

Oxford University Press, Ely House, London W.1

GLASGOW NEW YORK TORONTO MELBOURNE WELLINGTON
CAPE TOWN SALISBURY IBADAN NAIROBI LUSAKA ADDIS ABABA
BOMBAY CALCUTTA MADRAS KARACHI LAHORE DACCA
KUALA LUMPUR SINGAPORE HONG KONG TOKYO

MADE AND PRINTED IN GREAT BRITAIN BY
WILLIAM CLOWES AND SONS, LIMITED
LONDON AND BECCLES

PREFACE

This is a (considerably expanded) version of what I gave as the Gregynog lectures at the University of Wales (Aberystwyth) in November 1967. It was the invitation to give those lectures which acted as the catalyst, precipitating something which, I now realize, had long been brewing in my mind.

I am not an economic historian, but I have long been interested in economic history; and there are some of the most eminent among economic historians from whom I have been able, personally, to learn. When I was a postgraduate student, my supervisor was G. D. H. Cole; and it was only a little after that (when I was 'on loan' to the University of the Witwatersrand, in South Africa) that I found myself lecturing on English mediaeval economic history—from the lecture notes of Eileen Power, lent to me to help me in that alarming part of the duties that fell upon me. As I followed through that story, having to put her vivid and intelligible account into my own words, a seed was sown, which may at last have germinated. Then came the talks I used to have with M. M. Postan, when we were both of us lecturers in London in the early thirties; I believe that he will recognize some of the things I learned from him in the following pages. But all that is long ago; I wandered away, and I am myself surprised to find that I have come back. I am sure I would not have done so, had it not been for T. S. Ashton. For seven years, at Manchester, we were the closest of colleagues; and later, after his retirement, I had him as a neighbour. Through him I could keep in touch with the circle of economic historians; I was encouraged to keep up my reading in the *Economic History Review*, since I could discuss it with him; I was even encouraged to develop views of my own, since I could argue them with him. He did not live to see my *Industrial Revolution* chapter, in its final form, and I do not know whether he would have approved of it; but much of the work that went into this book was discussed with him, at various stages.

During the time that I have been writing, I have had help from many others also. I have lectured it, not only at Aberystwyth but elsewhere; every time I have picked up something, criticism, example or idea, of which I have been able to make use. When I had no more than a couple of chapters, I gave them as papers to a seminar at Canberra; the Aberystwyth lectures were repeated in Oxford; and when the book was nearly complete, I gave it as lectures in Vienna. Something was gained from the discussions that followed on every one of these performances.

Most of those who helped me in these ways were economic historians or economists; but that was not enough. As I shall be explaining, I have tried to look at economic history in relation to other kinds of history, economic activities in relation to human activities of other sorts. I have not, at least in my own view, crossed the boundaries of economic history, but I have tried to go right up to those boundaries; and I could not do that without paying some attention to the things which lie beyond them. I count myself fortunate, for this reason in particular, that I was working in Oxford, and in All Souls College; so there were historians (and academic lawyers) whom I was meeting almost daily, and on whom I could call for advice when I needed it. There are so many of those who have helped me, sometimes on quite major matters, sometimes on quite small points; sometimes, I expect, without their realizing that they were helping me. It is difficult to draw a line. I have therefore refrained from explicit acknowledgement (save in one or two cases, where the reader might well wonder how I got hold of a journal which would obviously be no part of my regular reading). One cannot generalize, as I shall be trying to do, without making risky generalizations; I must take the full responsibility for them upon myself.

A note on the Index. There is a further point, which may usefully be mentioned here. I have tried, when writing, to keep several sorts of readers in mind. My former books have been read, by students of economics, in many countries; I hope this will also, but not only by students of economics. There are many things to which I shall be referring which will be obvious, and familiar, to some of these readers, not at all so familiar to others. How was I to help the latter, without annoying the former? I have tried to find an answer by extending the functions of an Index. It is a bigger index than one would expect to find in a book of this size, for it is not just an index, it is also a dictionary, in particular a dictionary of dates. So if the reader feels that there is some allusion, in the text, on which he would like a little more information, he may be able to find it in the Index.

May 1969   J. R. H.

CONTENTS

I

THEORY AND HISTORY

THIS is a small book on a large subject—an enormously large subject. It extends, in one of its dimensions, over the whole world; in another, over the whole span of human history, from the 'dark backward and abysm of time', the earliest ages of which anthropologists and archaeologists have given us some fragmentary knowledge, right up to that edge of the unknown future, the present day. I call it economic history; but I am not interpreting economic history in a narrow sense. I am certainly not claiming that it envelops the whole of history, or that one should always be looking for economic motives behind apparently non-economic behaviour; but I do not want to contract its boundaries, as is so often done in these days with the boundaries of economics itself. In spite of the vogue of 'Quantitative Economic History', economic historians are under less temptation than economists to see their subject as purely quantitative. This is not only for the reason that as we go back in time the figures become so patchy; there is a deeper reason, too. We are bound to find, as we go back into the past, that the economic aspects of life are less differentiated from other aspects than they are today. Economic history is often presented, and rightly presented, as a process of specialization; but the specialization is not only a specialization among economic activities, it is also a specialization of economic activities (what are becoming economic activities) from activities of other sorts. This is a specialization which is not yet complete and can never be complete; but it has gone far enough for us to imitate it in our studies. We contract the boundaries of our subjects, and of our sub-subjects, to make them more manageable; and we are enabled to do this because our academic specialization corresponds to something which is in fact happening in the 'real world'. But it is not all that is happening in the world; we suffer, and we know that we suffer, by getting so far apart. A major function of economic history, as I see it, is to be a forum where economists and political scientists, lawyers, sociologists, and historians—historians of events and of ideas and of technologies—can meet and talk to one another.

What I am hoping to do in this book is no more than to make a contribution to that conversation. That is why it can, after all, be a small book. It is also why (beginning, as I do, as an economist) it can be theory.

In what sense can one attempt a 'theory of history'? Theory and history, many would say, are opposites; at best, alternatives; it is not the business of a historian to think in theoretical terms. Or perhaps it would be conceded that he may make use of some disconnected bits of theory to serve as hypotheses for the elucidation of some particular historical processes; no more than that. I think I understand this scepticism, and I have some sympathy with it. I have more sympathy with it than with the grand designs of a Toynbee or a Spengler, the makers of historical patterns which have more aesthetic than scientific appeal. My 'theory of history' will quite definitely not be a theory of history in their sense. It will be a good deal nearer to the kind of thing that was attempted by Marx, who did take from his economics some general ideas which he applied to history, so that the pattern which he saw in history had some extra-historical support. That is much more the kind of thing I want to try to do.

It does not seem unreasonable to suppose that we can draw from social science, not only (in view of what has just been said) from economics, some general ideas which can be used by historians as a means of ordering their material. I suppose that most historians are coming to grant that this is so. What remains an open question is whether it can only be done on a limited scale, for special purposes, or whether it can be done in a larger way, so that the general course of history, at least in some important aspects, can be fitted into place. Most of those who take the latter view would use the Marxian categories, or some modified version of them; since there is so little in the way of an alternative version that is available, it is not surprising that they should. It does, nevertheless, remain extraordinary that one hundred years after *Das Kapital*, after a century during which there have been enormous developments in social science, so little else should have emerged. Surely it is possible that Marx was right in his vision of logical processes at work in history, but that we, with much knowledge of fact and social logic which he did not possess, and with another century of experience at our disposal, should conceive of the nature of those processes in a distinctly different way.

One of the things which we have learned—a general point which must be emphasized at the outset—is to distinguish between those historical questions which can usefully be discussed in terms of the notion of statistical uniformity, and those which cannot. Every historical event has some aspect in which it is unique; but nearly always there are other aspects in which it is a member of a group, often of quite a large group. If it is one of the latter aspects in which we are interested, it will be the group, not the individual, on which we shall fix our attention; it will be the average, or norm, of the group which is what we shall be trying to explain. We shall be able to allow that the individual may diverge from the norm without being deterred from the recognition of a statistical uniformity. This is what we do, almost all the time, in economics.[1] We do not claim, in our demand theory for instance, to be able to say anything useful about the behaviour of a particular consumer, which may be dominated by motives quite peculiar to himself; but we do claim to be able to say something about the behaviour of the whole market—of the whole group, that is, of the consumers of a particular product. We can do this, it must be emphasized, without implying any 'determinism'; we make no question that each of the con-

---

[1] When we stop doing so, as sometimes happens in the 'theory of the firm', we get into trouble.

sumers, as an individual, is perfectly free to choose. Economics is rather specially concerned with such 'statistical' behaviour.

The historical phenomena to which a theory of history might apply are those which, in the light of our interest in them, can be regarded as having this statistical character. Most of the phenomena of economic history (however widely considered) do have it; the questions we want to ask about economic history deal mainly with groupings that can be made to possess it. But the distinction is not, in principle, a distinction between economic and other kinds of history. In any department of history we may find ourselves looking for statistical uniformities. The distinction is between an interest in general phenomena and an interest in particular stories. Whenever our interest is in general phenomena, theory (economic or other social theory) may be relevant; otherwise usually not.

To take some examples. Suppose we take the view (which on some versions is quite a tempting view) that there would have been no French Revolution if Louis XVI had not been so lazy and inattentive[1]—that it could have been avoided if he had just had the virtues of a conscientious civil servant, like his ancestors Louis XIV or Philip II of Spain—then the French Revolution, regarded from that angle, would be a particular story, not one of the phenomena to which historical theory could be applied. Even so, it might be regarded from other angles from which it would look different. If we re-garded it as an expression of social changes, which would have occurred in France even under a better ruler, and which did occur in other countries in less spectacular ways, it would become a particular instance of a more general phenomenon, which could be theoretically discussed. Or if our interest were in the reasons for this concentration of power, which made it possible for the defects of one man to have such disastrous consequences, that again could be made into a theoretical question, though it would be even less of an economic question than the former. But these are relatively sophisti-

[1] 'He was bored with his job (son métier l'ennuyait)', so Madelin puts it (*La Révolution*, Paris 1933, p. 29).

cated questions which go much below the surface of the fact of the French Revolution.

As an obvious contrast, consider the 'Industrial Revolution' in England, the change in the organization of industry in England which was going on at much the same time. Some of the story of that Revolution can be told, and has been told, in particular biographies; but there is no biography that is central. No one would dream of claiming that there was any one particular man, any single inventor or entrepreneur, without whose activity the English Industrial Revolution could not have occurred.[1] Though there is a sense in which the Industrial Revolution is an event, it is itself a statistical phenomenon; it is a general tendency to which theory is unmistakably relevant.

A theory of history, such as I shall be trying to construct, will have to be concerned with such general phenomena; it is to history conceived in that way that it will have to apply. Such is by no means the whole of history; I have tried to make it quite clear that I do not think it is. There is another kind, which is not concerned with such general issues; which makes it a virtue to run in terms of individuals, their deeds, their characters, their relations with one another. It has to be concerned (too much for some modern tastes) with famous people; for it is only such people who have left enough record behind them for it to be possible for us to bring ourselves into personal contact with them. Sometimes we can get it directly, through their own writings; sometimes only indirectly, when enough is left for them to be brought back to life by the dramatic skill of historian or biographer. I am sure that kind of history should not be undervalued. It is relevant, even here; for it is unsafe to exercise one's imagination on the past— even to the extent that is needed for 'theoretical' purposes— unless it has been warmed by that 'old-fashioned' history.[2]

---

[1] There is an enjoyable attempt by an economic historian to tell a good part of the story of the American Industrial Revolution biographically. (J. R. T. Hughes, *The Vital Few*, Boston 1966). But I do not think (and I do not suppose that Professor Hughes would think) that it invalidates my point.

[2] Though the passage from the old style of history-writing (such as Macaulay's) to the new (of which the new *Cambridge Modern History* is an outstanding example)

After all, the way in which the economist develops his hypotheses is by asking himself the question: 'What should I do if I were in that position?' It is a question that must always be qualified by adding: 'if I were that kind of person'. If I were a mediaeval merchant, or a Greek slave-owner! It is only by getting a feel of what people were like that one can begin to guess.

The task which lies before us can now be described. It is a theoretical enquiry, which must proceed in general terms— the more general the better. We are to classify states of society, economic states of society; we are to look for intelligible reasons for which one such state should give way to another. It will be a sequence not altogether unlike the 'Feudalism, Capitalism, Socialism' of Marx, or the stages of economic development of the German Historical School.[1] But our presuppositions are less deterministic, less evolutionary than theirs, and that will make a difference. It is only a *normal* development for which we are looking, so it does not have to cover all the facts; we must be ready to admit exceptions, exceptions which nevertheless we should try to explain. We are not to think of our normal process as one which, on being begun, is bound to be completed; it may be cut short from external causes, or it may encounter internal difficulties from which only sometimes there is a way of escape. All these possibilities will be admitted. Though we distinguish an underlying trend to which we may be willing to give the name of

may seem to bring the historian nearer to the economist, it is not an unmixed advantage even from the latter's point of view. It is so easy for the economist to forget that the 'actors' in his models (if the models are to be practically useful) should have at least one characteristic of real people, that they do not know what is going to happen; so they must take their decisions in the light of possibilities that look as if they might be realized, but which (as we now know from hindsight) are not going to be realized. Diplomatic history may seem at first sight to be the department of history which is furthest removed from economics; but since it is in the documents of diplomatic history that contingency planning is at its most explicit, it has lessons for the economist. I shall try to remember those lessons in the pages that follow.

[1] For a classical criticism of the views of the German Historical School (so influential around 1900), see W. Eucken, *Grundlagen der Nationalökonomie* (Godesberg 1947) Ch. 4.

'progress' or 'growth' or 'development', it is progress that is often interrupted, and which only too often takes disagreeable, even terrible forms. After all, why not? We are accustomed to thinking of our last two centuries as a period of economic development, but it is a development that has been irregular ('cyclical') and has many dark places to it. Why should the same not hold further back?

Every statistical time-series can be analysed, by purely mechanical methods, into trend and cycle; it is a natural human way of thinking, applicable, in a rough way, to non-numerical data also. Why should we not treat the Economic History of the World as a single process—a process that (at least so far) has a recognizable trend? Even the rises and declines of civilizations can find a place among the cycles that are imposed upon it.

Where shall we start? There is a transformation which is antecedent to Marx's Rise of Capitalism, and which, in terms of more recent economics, looks like being even more fundamental. This is the Rise of the Market, the Rise of the Exchange Economy. It takes us back to a much earlier stage of history, at least for its beginnings; so far back indeed that on those beginnings (or first beginnings) we have little direct information. But there are several ways in which we can deduce, fairly reliably, what must have occurred.

It is evident, in the first place, that the transformation was a gradual transformation; some of its later stages come much more clearly into the light of day. Secondly, it was not a transformation that occurred once for all; there are societies which have slipped back from being exchange economies, after which the same tale has been gone through again. Thirdly, there are 'underdeveloped' countries which have only undergone the transformation in quite recent times; some, even now, have not completed it. From these various sources we have a good deal of indirect evidence; so that we can fairly safely deduce what must have happened, for the first time, many centuries B.C.

My plan is that we begin with this transformation, that we seek to define it, and then see, so far as we can, what logically follows from it. We shall look over our shoulders at the historical record, so as to see that we do not put our logical process into a form which clashes with the largest and most obvious facts. (This is only the first stage of fitting, but it is as far as we shall go.) As we continue with the implications, many things, we shall find, will fit into place. We can continue the sequence (subject to the qualifications that have been mentioned) right up to the rise of Industrialism, and to the reaction against the market which has followed (or appears to have followed) upon it. But we shall not be able (as a deterministic theorist might think he was able) to extrapolate into the future; all we shall be able to do, all the economist is ever able to do, is to speculate about things which, more or less probably, may happen. Even that will be left, for nearly the whole of this book, severely aside.

II

CUSTOM AND COMMAND

I HAVE said that the Rise of the Market was a transformation; what was it that was being transformed? What was there before? We cannot hope to understand the transformation process unless we begin by getting some notion on this essential point.

There was a stage in the development of economics (most of us were still at that stage when I myself began to study economics in the nineteen-twenties) when economists were so wrapped up in market economics that they were unwilling to contemplate anything else—unwilling to grant that there was any other organization which could ever be a serious alternative. Markets might be more or less 'perfect'; it was the business of the economist to look for ways of making them as perfect as possible. Since that time there has been a great change. Partly through the experience of war-time, partly from observation of what has been happening in 'centrally planned economies', partly because of some purely theoretical developments (in Welfare Economics and in Linear Programming), we have learned that non-market organization has to be taken much more seriously. It has become standard practice to work with comparisons between market organization and non-market organization: to use non-market organization as a standard of reference by which the market is to be judged. But the non-market organization, thus used as a standard, is itself taken to be a 'perfect' organization; and a perfect non-market organization is as unrealistic as a perfect market. The non-market organization which we shall need, in order to begin our sequence sensibly, must be very 'imperfect'. In what would its imperfection consist? In what must it consist?

If the wants of society formed a single self-consistent system (such as could be expressed in an indifference map or in a 'Social Welfare Function'), and if all the decisions about provisions to meet those wants were taken by a single decider, it would only be necessary that the single decider should take the 'right' decisions, and the Social Optimum would be attained. This is the model we use in our textbooks, and for appropriate purposes it has its place. But it is not what happens, even in a centrally planned economy. It is not what can happen. The perfect organization, in this sense, is not really an organization at all.

There was, in the old days, a famous definition of Socialism: 'A little Webb sitting in the middle of a big web.' That indeed would have been an organization. The little Webb would have spent his time devising teams and committees, working with management charts. He would in fact have been operating, on a large scale, like the manager of a factory. The factory, though it is producing for the market, buying and hiring from the market, is a non-market organization *in its internal structure*. We can get some hints, from the management structure of the ordinary factory, of what a non-market production organization quite necessarily is.

It is quite clear that the manager does not make all the decisions himself. There is delegation of decision-making. Only some decisions are made centrally; the rest are left to be made by the lower orders in the hierarchy. The need for delegation is commonly explained in terms of limited capacity for oversight. The manager cannot 'be everywhere at once'; and he cannot know everything at once. That by itself is a sufficient reason for delegation. But it is probable that there is a further reason. The power to take decisions, even over a limited field, is a thing on which the normal person sets considerable value; he has to be called on to be something more than a mere automaton if he is to give of his best. He needs, at the least, a little freedom to do his own job his own way. It is only by the most iron discipline that he can be deprived of that freedom. Why should one take the trouble to exercise such pressure, unless it is needed? It is simpler to delegate.

If the delegation of decision-making is not to lead to chaos, it must proceed by rule. There must be rules which circumscribe the fields in which individuals are free to take decisions; rules which will commonly take the form of prescribing the place of the individual in the organization. They may be written rules; but for the most part they are understandings, implications of the job the individual is set, which will serve in the place of written rules (or as a supplement to written rules) if they are understood well enough. A production unit (such as our factory) may be defined in terms of the things it produces, of the capital that is embodied in it, or of the labour that is employed to work it; but we get nearer to its essence if we regard it as an *organization*, now revealed as a structure of rules and understandings, the rules and understandings by which the various grades in its hierarchy are fitted together.

An organization, so conceived, is like a living thing. If it was entirely reducible to written rules it would not be a living thing, only a formula; but this again is an extreme case that does not occur. Even written rules require to be interpreted and applied to particular cases; and there is no way in which they can be interpreted except in terms of previous experience. As for understandings, the more informal an understanding is, the more it must rely upon precedent; the more dependent it accordingly is upon continuity over time. It is impossible that an organization should be entirely handed down as a blueprint from above. It has to grow, being based at every moment on what has gone before.

Like living things, organizations can die, and they can be born. A new organization may have new rules, and these may differ extremely from any that have been previously observed. But even new rules require to be interpreted, and the way in which they are interpreted depends upon the environment into which they are introduced. Even across Revolutions, there is some degree of continuity. In an organization which has settled down into what, by analogy, we may call 'equilibrium', the continuity will be very great.

What has all this to do with the problem that I began by posing: how should we conceive of the *primitive* non-market organization, from which the transformation, which I called the Rise of the Market, was to set out? From what I have been saying, about things much nearer home, we can perhaps derive some useful hints.

The system of rules and understandings which (according to this analysis) is present to this day in the ordinary firm, is designed to a large extent 'from the top'. To a large extent, but not wholly. For the rules must be such as to be understood by those who are to work them; and not only understood but, at least in the main, accepted. (An organization whose rules are not accepted can hardly be 'in equilibrium'.) The designer, or builder, of a viable firm does not have a free hand; he is restricted, not only by the regular economic scarcities, but also by the kinds of conditions that are acceptable, or can by some means be made acceptable, to those with whom he is to work.

Thus the rules come in part from 'above' and in part from 'below'; the proportions of 'aboveness' and 'belowness' in viable rules may differ very much in different circumstances. Even though it may be possible to distinguish a 'chain of command', by which orders are transmitted from one grade in the hierarchy to another, it will be found, on examination, that the orders which any particular individual will expect to receive from his superiors are not any orders, but orders of a particular kind, or kinds. In an organization which is inclined to 'belowness', the orders that can be passed on from one grade to another will be narrowly restricted. Though such an organization may be able to perform some limited functions quite adequately, it will be inflexible. It will be unable to respond to new emergencies, emergencies that differ in some essential respect from those that have been previously experienced. It is hardly possible for an organization to respond to a new emergency without some central decision, and a central decision that can be made effective; thus in an organization (such as an army) which is continually being required to make certain kinds of new adjustments, the share of 'aboveness' in its system of control must be very great. But even in an army there is a distinction between the kinds of commands which his subordinates will normally respect to receive from a commanding officer, commands which are consistent with the retention by them of their normal places in the organization; and commands of a different character which involve reorganization. Even in an army commands of this latter character—the extreme of 'aboveness'—will be relatively rare.

Consider, at the other extreme, the case of a community of people who are not much disturbed in their ancient ways by external pressures. Their economy can function, with every member performing his allotted task, including the decision-making which is left to him within his allotted circle; over-riding decisions 'from the centre' will scarcely ever have to be made. Once such a system has attained an equilibrium, it can continue for long ages without the need for reorganization—without the need for new decisions of an organizational character. The ordinary emergencies, such as harvest failures or attacks by the 'usual' enemies, would not require new decisions; ways of dealing with them could be incorporated within the traditional rules. So long as this equilibrium persisted, there might even be no need for an organ by which ultimate authority could be exercised. If the emergency arose, authority would have to be improvised; but until the emergency arose, it would not have to be decided where it lay.

Surely it is along this line that we must construct our model (or rather, as we shall see, one of our models) of the primitive non-market economy from which our story is to begin. 'Customary' economies, which answer more or less to this description, do indeed seem to be well identifiable; they are known to historians and (especially) to anthropologists. The economy of a neolithic or early mediaeval village, as well as of the tribal communities which have survived until lately in many parts of the world, was not organized by its Ruler (if such existed); it was based upon a corpus of tradition. By that tradition individual function was prescribed, and continued to be prescribed. It is important to emphasize that the 'head' of the organization (King or Chief or High Priest or Council of Elders) would himself be a part of the traditional structure. He also would have prescribed functions, together with appropriate rights that would go with them.

The most perfect examples of such customary organization are those that have been investigated by anthropologists; it is probable that this is significant. We can understand that it is people who have hidden themselves away in long inaccessible places who are most rarely confronted with new emergencies; so that their customary organization, established (no doubt) in the first place by slow degrees, can persist for long periods almost undisturbed. But these are the peoples who have inhabited the by-ways of history; for those who are on the main roads there are other possibilities. Long before the Rise of the Market, quite independently of all that development, they will have been confronted with new emergencies; if they are not to be overwhelmed, they must respond by evolving some more positive leadership. All that may sometimes be required is a single reorganization, after which the community can carry on in a customary manner that in some respect has been changed. But when the reorganization required is more complex or more drastic, it will itself take time; and the community will have to be organized in a new way, during the period of reorganization. It is almost inevitable that during that period the command which emanates from a centre will become the distinguishing characteristic. The other pure form of the non-market economy is therefore the command economy, which in its primitive shape will almost inevitably have a military character. When a customary economy is sufficiently disturbed, it will pass right over to a military despotism. The Bantu villages throw up a Chaka, the Mongol nomads a Genghiz Khan.

What are the kinds of disturbance which may have such effects? It is tempting to answer the question on economic lines, in terms of population pressure. This is a possible answer, but it should not be assumed that it is the only answer. The peoples who have maintained themselves in customary equilibrium for long periods must have found some way of containing population pressure; why should not others have done likewise? It can only be because they have passed through a stage in which such control was not necessary. If population increases, land requirements increase; there must therefore have been a stage in which there was ample land, permitting an increase of population under a system of land usage which goes on long enough to become traditional. Even so, a point will come when the land which is suitable for food production by traditional methods is fully occupied, so that the people of one tribe begins to encroach upon the land that is used by its neighbours. As the encroachment develops, it builds up into a real and continuing threat. That is certainly one of the ways in which the 'revolution' may come about; but we should be careful not to jump to the conclusion that it is the only way. It is probably true that the only motive which can induce a people to substitute a revolutionary despotism for their traditional institutions is Fear; but there are many kinds of Fear. There is Fear of the Gods, as well as of human enemies. The motive, even today, and quite as much in early times, need not be so very rational. Thus there is no need to be dogmatic about the nature of the 'emergency'.

We have now two types: the customary economy and the command economy. But these are pure types, extreme types; it is entirely possible (and, as we shall see, very common) to be something in between. The despot is unlikely to destroy all kinds of custom; when the emergency is passed that gave him his opportunity, custom will creep back. A pure, or almost pure, command economy can hardly exist excepting in an emergency, for it is only in the emergency that a wide range of orders from the centre will be accepted. The case is the same as that in the firm, with which we began; some 'belowness' as well as some 'aboveness' is bound in the end to be a necessary part of its organization. In the emergency the community has become, to all intents and purposes, an army; but the time will come when the army has to be transformed into an instrument of civil government. This (many instances confirm) is a very difficult stage; it may happen that the empire fails to pass it, so that the central power, save perhaps in nominal terms, just disappears.[1] But even if the central power disappears, there may be consolidation at a lower level. Failure may not be complete failure; but success may not be complete success.

The multitude of systems of social organization to which the term 'feudalism' has been applied—including those to which many would say it is misapplied—have perhaps no more than one thing in common. They are a low degree of success in the transmutation of an army into a civil government. The generals are made governors of provinces, the captains their district officers. They retain some memory of the positions from which they have sprung, so they have still some feeling of allegiance to the centre; but the power of the centre to enforce its commands upon them has become very limited, so that hardly more authority over them is retained than is expressed in some customary rights. This is the position of the centre over against the great lords; and there is the same pattern in the relation of the great lords to lesser lords, who were formerly their subordinates. The system has reverted to custom; little more is left of the command element than the fact that custom is expressing itself in hierarchy.

That is feudalism expressed in organizational terms; but there is an economic aspect also which is very characteristic. Already at the stage of military despotism there was a problem of supplying the armies. If the army was attacking, it could be supplied by plunder; this simple solution of the supply problem has been a temptation to aggressors in all ages. But even a successful aggressor will come to the point where he has to defend his conquests; supply by plunder is never an ultimate solution. The point will come when the army, or at least some nucleus of armed force, needs regular support— when it is necessary for the despot to assure himself of a regular income. There are two ways in which he can do this:

[1] An obvious example is the break-up of the Macedonian Empire after the death of Alexander. More often, however, for reasons which we shall see in a moment, the break-up is somewhat delayed. But it may be little delayed, as was the case (to take a recent example) with the dissolution of the Fulani empire into the Northern Nigerian emirates.

by setting captives to work as slaves, or by imposing contributions (the ancestors of our taxes) upon his subjects. We are
accustomed to thinking of one of these methods as barbaric,
the other as civilized; but at the stage with which we are concerned in this chapter they slide into one another. Is forced
labour part-time slavery, or is it a form of tax-payment? It
can be looked at either way.

Even a slave has to live; it is always part, and not the whole,
of a slave's economic product that can be taken from him. It is
only too true that so much may be taken that productivity
declines, or that the slave population fails to reproduce itself
in the longer run. It is not only the material possessions (the
crops and herds) of the conquered that may be plundered;
their human productive power may be plundered too. But
one does not get a regular income by plunder, and it is a
regular income that in the end is required. If the military
economy (or that which succeeds it) is to find an equilibrium,
enough must be left to the slaves, or to the 'contributors', for
them to survive and to continue to produce.

I have introduced taxation (or 'contribution') in terms of
military despotism; but taxation that is bearable does not
need to have force behind it. There is a place for contribution,
even in the purest form of customary economy; there must
be, as soon as there is any class that does not support itself by
the work of its hands. As soon as there are priests and elders,
they have to be supported; but they can readily be supported
by customary offerings. We should think of the despot's taxes
as becoming absorbed into the same customary system. They
become rights to which he is entitled; they are assimilated to
the offerings that are made to Religion.

From the revenues that are paid to the King he has to
support his servants: his army in the first place, any other
servants he may have after that. Now there is here—the point
is extremely important when communications are difficult—a
problem of transfer. The contributions are paid in kind, in
direct labour services, or (very generally) in agricultural
produce. For this reason alone it is very easy to slip into
feudalism. For when the army has dispersed, to govern the

provinces, sub-provinces and districts of which the kingdom is composed, those who are to be supported out of the revenue to be collected are likely to be nearer to the sources of revenue than it is possible for a central government to be. Slaves may well be brought from great distances for particular works (for such undertakings as the building of the Pyramids or of the Great Wall of China); but it is horribly wasteful of labour to carry labour for great distances when it is not necessary to do so, and the same will hold for unnecessary transport of agricultural produce. To carry produce to the centre and then back, in order that the King's representatives on the spot should have their share of the produce, the share which they need for their support, is so wasteful as to be absurd. It is vastly easier to allow the local lords to take their share on the way, so that it is only the residue, after they have taken what is due to them, which comes to the centre. But on this plan it will be the local lords who collect the contributions; all that is left to the centre is what they choose, or think proper, to hand over to it. This is feudalism in its economic aspect. It is easy to see how under pure feudalism, from this economic cause alone, the centre is in the long run in danger of withering away.

Against this erosion of his power (of his economic and therefore of his political power) a strong and determined ruler will naturally struggle. But what is the alternative? There is only one alternative: he must create a civil administration, a bureaucracy or civil service. This bureaucratic solution is more difficult, more sophisticated, than the feudal. It will only develop its full potentialities when the market institutions, the evolution of which I shall be considering in later chapters, have come to strengthen it; but it is in principle independent of market institutions, so it belongs in this place. There is indeed evidence, from the historical record, that the beginnings of the evolution of bureaucracy go back to very early times.

How does one distinguish bureaucracy from the military command system, which (as we saw) was so inclined to slip into feudalism? The feudal magnates themselves had begun by being royal servants or subordinates; a mere change of name would not prevent the civil administrators from following in the same track. The most necessary function of these new civil servants would be the collection of revenue. But they again have to be supported out of this same revenue; there is the same danger of erosion of revenue from their operations as there was in the case of the feudal lords. If bureaucracy is really to be an answer, it needs to be fortified. The defences, which experience seems to have shown to be necessary, are three in number.

The first of the conditions for success is that servants should be employed to keep a watch, or check, on other servants: a check which in its primitive, arbitrary, form is mere spying, but which can be reduced to rule, so that it can grow (at a later stage) into such things as the audit system of modern bureaucracies. A division of function between military and civil officers, so that (in particular) the collection of revenue is taken out of the hands of the military, is an example of this check—an outstandingly important example. A system of promotion—or just moving-around—which prevents particular individuals from acquiring the independence which almost necessarily follows from long-continued exercise of the same office, is a second condition. A system of recruitment, by which the bureaucracy is continually refreshed by new entrants, deliberately selected for suitable qualities, so that it does not settle down into an inherited caste, is a third.

These are difficult conditions, but the earliest attempts to satisfy them are very ancient. Probably the oldest biography of a civil servant that has come down to us is the inscription on the tomb of a certain Weni,[1] who was 'overseer of the tenants of the Palace' (should one say 'controller of the King's household'?) in sixth dynasty Egypt (about 2300 B.C.). It would appear from Weni's story that there already existed a system of promotion, and a system of recruitment (Weni records that he had a humble origin); but the first of the conditions just listed does not seem to have been observed at all regularly, for Weni, though his employments were mainly

[1] Sir Alan Gardiner, *Egypt of the Pharaohs* (Oxford 1961), pp. 94–7.

civil, was put on one important occasion in command of an army. Ancient Egypt may thus be regarded as having the elements of bureaucracy (as witnessed by this and similar instances), sufficient to explain the many-centuries-long persistence of a centralized state—'one of the best-organized civilisations the world has ever seen.'[1] Lapse into feudalism was nevertheless a continual danger. Offices tended to become hereditary, and the appearance of a provincial nobility was not unknown.[2]

Another remarkable example of successful bureaucracy (much later in date, but deserving mention here, because of the curious parallels between it and the Egyptian) is the traditional bureaucracy of Imperial China. It goes back, at least, to the time of the Han dynasty (contemporary with the Roman Empire); it lasted until less than a hundred years ago, and has clearly left deep traces upon the systems that have succeeded it. The principles of bureaucracy were well understood by the Chinese; they were made much more explicit by the Chinese than they seem ever to have been by the Egyptians. Most remarkable of all was the Chinese system of recruiting the mandarin class by competitive examination.[3] Such successful bureaucracy did indeed attain an 'equilibrium', a very stable equilibrium. It could sustain violent shocks (such as the Mongol invasion of the thirteenth century A.D.) and could restore itself after the shock to very much what it was before.

These are the great examples of 'classical' bureaucracy; anything so successful as this is elsewhere most uncommon.[4] The more usual pattern, after initial establishment, is disintegration, or a slide into feudalism, which may itself be no more than a step to disintegration. A characteristic example is the Mogul Empire in India. In its great days, under Akbar

[1] Gardiner, op. cit. p. 106.

[2] Ibid., pp. 90, 105.

[3] E. O. Reischauer and J. K. Fairbank, *East Asia: the Great Tradition* (New York 1958), pp. 106, 304–6.

[4] The Peru of the Incas may be another example. Modern European bureaucracies (and their imitators) belong, as we shall see (pp. 97–100 below), to a different type.

and Jahangir, it could pass as a 'classical' bureaucracy, like those of Egypt and China; but long before the British came on the scene, it had slipped. The Nawabs and Nizams had originally been servants of the Emperor; but by the eighteenth century their allegiance had become no more than nominal. Again, it may happen that the bureaucracy is able to maintain itself, but only over a limited area, much narrower than that which it purports to control. A Royal domain from which the Monarch draws substantial revenues, surrounded by feudal estates, over which his control is very sketchy, is a common pattern; it is familiar in mediaeval Europe, and it recurs in substantially the same shape in seventeenth- and eighteenth-century Japan.[1]

If the first beginnings of the Market are put back to the early date which is probably necessary, all of these examples (even that of 'Old Kingdom' Egypt) are subsequent to these first beginnings; yet I think it is justifiable to use them in this place. For the processes which we have been analysing are logically independent of the Market. They can occur without significant market development, and when they have occurred at later dates, such market development as had already occurred can have had little to do with them. They do thus give us the answer to the question I began by asking, of the nature of the non-market economy on which the new forces, which I shall be considering in later chapters, will be going to impinge. It is, after all, not such a simple answer. There are the two pure types: the customary economy with its complete 'belowness' and the command economy with its complete 'aboveness'—and there are the mixed types that come between. Feudalism is a mixed type, in which custom has become dominant; classical bureaucracy is another mixed type, in which the command element is relatively stronger. Under the pressure of what Toynbee would call a 'challenge' the system may swing in the command direction; but in the absence of challenge there is a law of inertia, a kind of social gravitation, which has the opposite effect. The performance of particular functions and the enjoyment of corresponding

[1] Sir G. Sansom, *History of Japan*, vol. III (London 1964), esp. Ch. 5.

privileges become rights, to which people (and groups of people) come to think themselves entitled. And since inheritance is the simplest way by which such rights can be passed on, they tend to become hereditary. Hereditary aristocracy, and specialization into trades by inherited caste, are equally examples of this same 'gravitation' phenomenon.

These forms of society differ, but there is one thing—one strictly economic thing—which all of them (save perhaps the purest customary type) have in common. Their central economic nexus is revenue: the tax, or tribute, or land rent (for in the absence of a market, these are not distinguished) which is paid by the peasant or cultivator, the producer of food, to some recognized authority. Perhaps one should hardly admit the exception, for even if political authority is absent, there are likely to be some religious contributions which work the same way. The nearer the approach to centralization and command, the more important the revenue will potentially become. In a bureaucratically controlled empire, revenue may be highly concentrated. In feudal systems it is dispersed, but the revenues of greater and even of lesser lords may still be sufficiently concentrated to have a momentous effect. For it is here, before there is any market (or without any dependence upon a market) that we first meet a substantial opportunity for specialization and division of labour. There is indeed some specialization, as between sexes and age-groups, even in the most primitive tribe; but it is not the deliberate and creative specialization which concentration of revenue makes possible. We have already noticed one form of specialization which comes in at this point—the specialization of function which is a necessary condition for efficient bureaucracy; but as this develops, other kinds of specialization are likely to develop with it. The Ruler need not confine himself to using his revenue to supply his army and his tax-collectors; when the emergency is passed, there are more attractive ends to which some of it can be devoted. To surround himself with splendour is not only attractive in itself; it is a way of maintaining his authority. The 'vicarious consumption' which he thus permits his subjects, is a way of 'winning the hearts of his people'.

> With rich perfume in every room delightful to that princely train,
> Which again *we* shall see, when the time it shall be
> That the King enjoys his own again

goes the Royalist song. It is only too true that the luxury which delights the prince may be burdensome to his subjects, while that which delights his subjects may be burdensome to the ruler. Up to a point, however, the two go together.

It is a poor form of splendour for the Ruler to surround himself with an undifferentiated multitude of servants. If the more ingenious of them are specialized upon particular tasks, they can become skilled; the glory is yet more glorious when it is adorned, as it can then be, with miracles of craftsmanship. What are the oldest artistic productions which remain to us, and which we still regard as indisputably of the first rank? Surely it is the sculpture of the Pyramid Age, of fourth dynasty Egypt. The men who made those things must have been servants of the Pharaohs. It was in such royal households (and in those attached to temples) that human intelligence, applied to the manual arts, and even beyond, first came into full flower.

We have been so accustomed, ever since Adam Smith, to the association of division of labour with market development, that it comes with something of a shock when one realizes that this was not its origin. The first development of skill is independent of the market. It does imply specialization, but it is a specialization (like that which occurs when a new process is introduced into a modern factory) that is directed from the top. Specialization is indeed a matter of the economies of scale; it does depend upon the concentration of demand; but the market is only one of the ways by which demand may be concentrated. There is another, which was already present, very mightily present, in the classical bureaucracies; and which even in the households of feudal lords was present to a not negligible extent.

This alternative description of the non-market economy as a Revenue Economy, in which a 'surplus' of food and other necessaries is extracted from cultivators, and used to provide sustenance for public servants, is the final point which I want to emerge from this chapter. It is a genuine form of economic organization, which is to be contrasted with the market form; it is the principal background against which the evolution of the market is to be studied. It precedes the market, but it has of course survived the market. Even in the heyday of *laissez-faire*, the Revenue Economy had by no means wholly disappeared. The State still had its servants, and they needed to be supplied. The growth of the Public Sector, in our day, is a massive swing-back towards the Revenue Economy. But it is to a Revenue Economy which, even its most socialist forms, has been profoundly transformed by experience of market forces. One of the ways in which they have transformed it is by offering it opportunities for economic calculation, which in the primitive Revenue Economy must have been almost wholly lacking. And though some of the reasons for the swing-back are military reasons, which are fundamentally not dissimilar to those which would swing the primitive Revenue Economy in a command direction, others are associated with a change in the character of the State, which could hardly have occurred excepting through the market experience.[1]

These are matters on which I shall be enlarging in much later chapters. We have first to examine how market institutions have evolved, out of the background which I have been describing. We may then be in a position to judge how far they have been able, or could conceivably have been able, to take over.

[1] The Revenue Economy has a peculiar place in the history of economic thought. It can readily be recognized in the system of ideas of the Physiocrats, the earliest group of economists to make an impression on public opinion—in France of the 1760s. The Physiocrats were dealing with an exchange economy; they knew that they were dealing with an exchange economy; they nevertheless resorted, in much of their thinking, to a model that goes back before exchange. Agriculture, in their view, was alone 'productive'; and why? Because it produced what the experience of ages had shown to be the taxable surplus (or so it seemed to them). Non-agricultural workers were a 'sterile class'—because, in this same experience, they seemed to be supported out of the expenditure of this surplus and did not contribute to it. Even the France of their day was outgrowing this pattern, but they had not outgrown it in their thinking. Their 'impot unique' was a recommendation of a return to it.

III

THE RISE OF THE MARKET

WE have now set our stage, and are ready for the entrance of our principal character. That he is a principal character there can be no question; but whether he is hero, or villain, or tragic hero, remains to be seen.

The background is the customary economy, made more or less hierarchical by a command element. It is an economy (we may take it) that already practises agriculture; it has government, which may be of a simple form, but may be quite sophisticated; it has industry, at least in the sense of handicraft. What it does not have, and what is going to be so important, is trade. There are farmers, and soldiers, and administrators, and craftsmen; but there are no traders, no one who is specialized upon trade.

I would emphasize that it is specialization upon trade which is the beginning of the new world; not the preliminary stages of trading without specialization. Casual trading—isolated acts of exchange, involving no commitment by either party that there will be further exchanges—such must have occurred, now and then, from the earliest times, but the effects on the lives of those making them will have been minimal. There is besides a kind of near-trading which must be ruled out, in spite of the deep mark which it has left on the archaeological record; it is entirely consistent with the *mores* of the simplest customary economy, so that from our point of view it marks no decisive change. There will be occasions, such as weddings, at which it is proper to give presents; and if presents are given one way, it is necessary for the preservation of dignity that they should be given in the other. The presents must be suitable, but there is no need for them to be in any recognizable sense equivalent. The wide dispersion, over areas inhabited by primitive peoples, of certain articles considered suitable for gifts (do we not know such articles nowadays?) needs no more than this to explain it.[1] The stage is far distant when a gift is expected to be 'new from the shop'; it will be none the worse for being second- or third-hand. Such interchange of gifts may be pre-trade; but it is not yet trade.

How does the trader—the specialized trader—come upon the scene? He cannot trade unless he has something to trade with; how does he get his stock? It is not easy to see that there is any way, within the normal working of a customary econo-my, by which he could get it; so it is tempting to conclude that he must have got it, in the first place, in some 'illicit' manner. He must have begun by being a pirate or brigand; otherwise he could not get started. Now it must certainly be admitted that this is one possible way in which he might begin. The receiver of stolen goods is one kind of trader; piracy and maritime trade have on occasion been curiously intertwined. There is, however, no reason to suppose that this is the principal answer. It only looks plausible that it should be because we are making a short cut. There is no reason why the specialized trader should come upon the scene all at once; there are more 'normal' ways in which he can find an en-trance if we allow him to be evolved.

On the way to the evolution of specialized trading comes the rise of regular trading. The simplest way in which regular trading may grow up is probably the following.

Any kind of social gathering (such as a religious festival) provides an opportunity for trading; trading which begins as casual, but becomes habitual. The articles may have been brought, in the first place, for personal consumption during the festival, or as gifts for the god; but if the participants do not bring just the same things, they will be tempted to barter with one another some of the goods they have brought. As this

[1] Grahame Clark, 'Traffic in Stone Axe and Adze Blades', *Economic History Review*, August 1965. I have been greatly helped, in the formulation of my ideas, by this stimulating article.

begins, it is a mere side-line; and if the advantages to be got from such rudimentary trading are small, it will remain a side-line.[1] But when the advantages are more considerable the new activity will grow; and it may well grow at the expense of that which was the original motive for meeting. The religious 'harvest festival' turns into a village fair.

Those who trade at such fairs will not yet, for the most part, be specialized traders. Even when trading has become habitual, and the market is open frequently, the traders may still be peasants who come to the market once a week; no more change in their way of life need be made than that. It is entirely possible for trading to continue for long ages in nothing more than this simple manner.[2] It is, nevertheless, no more than a short step from the fair to the beginning of specialized trading.

It may be that some of the peasants are richer than others, or simply that they have larger amounts of tradable goods than others have (not the same thing). Since they have more to sell, others will be particularly anxious to do business with them; their trade becomes more active. The goods which are offered to them will not always be goods which they themselves desire to acquire (simple barter presupposes a willingness to acquire on each side); but since their trade is more active, they will sometimes be willing to take such goods, because they have superior opportunities for passing them on to someone else. They are then beginning to act as middlemen,

[1] If the form of agriculture practised is solely (or almost solely) plant cultivation, and if the farms that are within reach of the market grow much the same crops, opportunities for advantageous exchange are likely to be small; variations in physical conditions within the area will of course make them more extensive. Advantages from exchange are perhaps more regularly attainable in the case of animal husbandry. Beasts die, and are born; if there are no exchanges the 'mix' of stock on the farm will frequently diverge, by these natural processes, from that which the farmer desires. By exchange he can get a better 'mix'.

[2] The country markets which survive to our day (even in Western Europe, and still more in 'underdeveloped' countries) are rarely 'pure' of the products of modern industry; their venerable antiquity is nevertheless easily recognizable. It is a thrill, after pushing one's way through the market which still flourishes in Urbino (central Italy) on Saturday mornings, to read the quotation from Montaigne which has been put up on a plaque on the city wall. He is describing his visit to Urbino in 1581; 'there was a market there, for it was Saturday.'

through whom exchanges can be arranged that are in effect multilateral. They may still be peasants as well as traders; but they are beginning to develop some partial specialization.

This can happen even at fairs that are quite infrequent; but when the market is open frequently, there is room for a further step. Goods that have been acquired for re-sale need not be re-sold on the same day; if they have some durability they can be held over and sold on a later occasion. The middleman who takes advantage of this opportunity has become a stock-holder; when that activity has become important to him, the safe-keeping of his stock becomes a major responsibility. To carry it to and fro between farm and market-place is both costly and risky; it will be safer to keep it at the market-place and watch over it there, being ready then (of course) to sell it at any time. When he has reached that point he has indeed become a specialized trader. He has changed his base of operations to the market-place; he has opened a shop.

Here, therefore, we have one route along which specialized trading may evolve; as we shall see, it is not the only such route. But before leaving it, let us take it one step further. It is not by any means necessary that while the stock which has been purchased for re-sale is being watched over, it should be preserved from material change. It must be preserved, so far as possible, from deterioration, from loss of saleability; but it may happen that by doing suitable work upon it, its sale-ability can be increased. The distinction between the pure trader, who buys to re-sell, to re-sell what is physically the same as what he had bought, and the artisan or 'producer' who works on the things he has bought, so as to re-sell them in a different form, is often regarded as fundamental; but economically, and even socially, it is not as fundamental as it looks. It is a technological, not an economic distinction. The shops of pure traders and the 'workshops' of artisans, 'pro-ducing' for the market, may exist (and in the days before industrialism commonly did exist) side by side.[1] The primitive 'manufacturer' (to use the old eighteenth-century word for

[1] One can still see them co-existing (even to this day) in a large oriental market, such as that of Isfahan.

him) was a craftsman, but he did not work for a master, like the craftsman we have already met in the Revenue Economy. He worked for the market. He bought and sold. He could not exist without buying and selling. He is therefore to be reckoned (as we shall reckon him) as one kind of specialized trader.[1]

I have now completed my account of one of the processes by which specialized trading might be evolved. It is a part of the explanation; but I do not think it is enough, by itself, to account for the transformation I have in mind. There is indeed a possible transition from this 'petit commerce' (as the French call it) to the 'grand commerce' which has a different kind of potentiality. The shopkeeper, as we have seen, makes the market continuous in time, by being ready to do business on any day, not just on market days. He may also do something to make it continuous in space, if he goes forth, or sends his agents to go forth, to fetch from neighbouring centres things he can profitably sell in his own centre, and for which he can offer in return things that are available in his own place. In this way trade can grow; it can grow gradually; but it seems unlikely that the 'grand commerce' has been built up solely in that manner.

There are other possibilities. The story I have so far been telling has begun from the customary economy of the village; we could however have begun from a form of society in which the element of command was stronger. In that society, as we have seen, specialization would already have been stronger. From an already achieved specialization there is a much readier access into relatively large-scale trade.

It can start right at the top. Any great King will be receiving embassies from neighbouring chieftains: some of them very small fry compared with himself, some his equals or near equals in power. They will bring presents which he will receive as tribute; but it will be beneath his dignity not to

---

[1] In adopting this classification, I am following the modern view (of Menger and Pareto), not that which Marx took from Adam Smith.

give presents in return.[1] There will be some among the things which are offered to him, of which he would like to have more. The easy way to get them is to send an embassy the other way, with gifts, and with instructions about the return gifts which will be acceptable. (In so doing, he is using the conventions of the customary economy, for a purpose which clearly runs outside those conventions; but surely we are at liberty to think of him doing this, for it is what he does in others of his activities also.)

The steward who is employed upon this task is already performing, by order, some of the functions of a merchant. If he performs them successfully, so that he is sent back for repeat performances, he will become specialized upon his new activity. He is not an independent merchant, but he is a merchant. He is still a servant of the King, a servant who (like other servants) has become specialized upon a particular function. Trading, on behalf of his master, is the function he is called on to perform.[2]

Though he is not an independent merchant, he will be scarcely distinguishable from an independent merchant in his particular dealings. He has to decide, for himself, whether or not to make a particular bargain; it is only for the general result of his trading, or for the result of a whole trading expedition, that he can be accountable. This being so, it is nearly inevitable, in the circumstances supposed, that he will pass over, to some extent, from his dependent status into independent merchanting. Perhaps he is being an 'unjust steward' when he takes his commission, keeping back some portion of the desirable objects he has been instructed to secure, so as to do a little private trading on his own. But he is not likely to see it that way, nor will his master do so; for he only appears to be doing the same as other servants are doing, who support themselves out of the revenues they collect, before handing on

[1] The scene is repeated, over and over again, on the Egyptian monuments. And one remembers how the Emperor of China (very naturally) took the first European merchants who came to his court to be bearers of tribute.

[2] Such, it may be supposed, were the merchants who worked for Solomon. 'And Solomon had horses brought out of Egypt, and linen yarn; and the king's merchants received the linen yarn at a price' (1 Kgs. 10:28).

what remains to the central Treasury. (He has, after all, to support himself while he is on his expedition; and why should he not do so in the most advantageous way?) The steward who acts in this way has already become a part-time independent merchant; just as in the former case, the new activity may gain on the old, so that it becomes in time the main activity.

I have told this second story in the grand way, where it may reckon as the beginning of international (or inter-regal) trade; but there is no reason why it should not repeat itself at lower levels. Lesser lords, and independent princelings, may be expected to engage, in what for them is substantially the same manner, in external trade. Whether they do so sufficiently for their servants to become specialized as merchants is a question of the advantage they can get from such trade as is available to them, on what they have to offer, and on the desirability of the goods which they can get in exchange from sources within reach. Even the ruler of a small territory, or the lord of a small estate, may find it worth while to specialize some of his servants on trading if the advantage that he can get from it is enough. (And we may be sure that he will then be under pressure from them to let them go shopping.)

So much for 'external' trade; but there is an internal trade that can grow up in a substantially similar way. The basis of the royal, or indeed of the feudal, economy is revenue; but revenue, paid in kind, will very normally (as we have seen) be paid in a form or at a place which is other than that at which authority desires to receive it. The craftsmen, whom we have found among the King's servants, must have materials on which to work; a part of the revenue (coming forward initially as food supply) must be diverted to meet the needs of those who are to supply the materials. These also (the miners or foresters) may be reckoned among the King' servants; but supplies to them will have to be organized, and it may well be easier to secure them by purchase from sources near at hand than to extract them by levies on the surrounding population. Those who organize supplies in this manner have opportunities that are similar to those of the steward who is engaged on external trade. There will indeed be many other opportunities for part-time merchanting arising from the collection and disposal of revenue. And part-time merchanting readily drifts into whole-time, as before.

All such trading, on behalf of a ruler (or minor lordling), will of course be immensely easier if markets, at which people are meeting to exchange produce, are already in existence; the two approaches to merchanting thus combine to fortify one another. The reinforcement works both ways. Cities, in their modern form, must largely be regarded as results of the transformation (or transformations) to which we are coming. The Ancient Monarchies did, however, have cities: cities which are only intelligible, as economic units, if we consider them to have been supported (or mainly supported) out of the expenditure of the revenue on which the economy of those societies was based. Memphis and Thebes, Nineveh and Nimrud and Babylon, Ch'ang-an and Lo-yang: they should surely be regarded, in the first place, as extended royal households, inhabited by the servants of the King, and the servants of those servants, and the servants of these, to many degrees.[1] There is, however, no doubt that they had markets. And it is easy to see, in the light of what has been said. that they must have had markets. These great concentrations of population (they were great concentrations of population) with an income, even in the form of raw produce, coming in to them from outside, had the wherewithal for many sorts of advantageous exchange. The traders on these markets would sometimes be 'escaped' peasants (like the traders in the village market with which we began); sometimes they would be 'escaped' servants of the nobility (like the steward who set up on his own account); sometimes they would be servants of the nobility who had only partially escaped. Already, at this early stage, the routes which we have been following out begin to run together.

We have now got our merchants, large or small, operating in one way or another, on the fringes of the customary or of

[1] They were government cities, like Washington was yesterday, and Canberra is to-day.

the command economy; and the transformation, which we are awaiting, has not yet fully occurred. But now we are ready for it. As soon as there is a class of merchants they will begin to form themselves, tightly or loosely, into a community, a community of a new type. It is a third type of organization which we have now to add to our customary and command types. We can hardly avoid labelling it *mercantile* or perhaps *commercial*; though the overtones which these words carry with them (especially when '-isms' are added to them) must be kept, at least for the present, well out of mind.

The mercantile economy is not at all a command economy; it is not 'planned'. By comparison with those we have been examining, it is highly individualistic; but that does not mean that it is anarchic. Even in their new capacity the merchants have organizational needs, and must find a way of meeting them. The economy which they are creating cannot develop far until they have grown some elements of a political, or quasi-political, structure that will fit it.

The simplest need—that for maintaining some sort of order in a crowded market-place—arises at once, but does not itself raise a new problem. Any government, even the pre-mercantile governments we have so far been considering, must set its face against brawling and rioting (or what count as brawling and rioting by its standards); for they present an obvious danger that is purely political. Meeting together on a market-place is one kind of assembly; every kind of assembly is potentially dangerous. This is the first reason for government intervention on the market; it explains why governments have so usually insisted upon markets being held under some sort of licence. But it is not necessary for mercantile transactions to take place in (potentially tumultuous) assemblies; the more regular dealings become, the less important this aspect is inclined to be.

Needs which are peculiar to the mercantile economy, and which do raise new problems, are chiefly two: the need for protection of property and the need for protection of contract.

I am not thinking so much of the need for protection of property against violence, though that comes in. It is one of the reasons why we find merchants clustering together in

towns and trading-posts, where they can join together to protect their property a little better than they could do on their
own. In this matter, even at the start, they have a common
interest. There is, in addition, a more 'legal' sense in which
they require a right of property.

The merchant must have property in the things in which he
trades; his right to that property must be identifiable. When
he sells an article he must be able to assure the buyer that the
thing is his to sell; he must be able to prove his property in
it, if he is challenged. This is not a thing which customary
institutions are at all well fitted to do for him. What right can
he have, in the eyes of a customary society, to things for which
he himself has no intelligible use? Things which he only
holds in order to get rid of them—to dispose of them, directly
or indirectly, to someone who does indeed have a need for
them? The right which he claims is a different right from that
of the peasant to his land, or of any family to its household
furniture, cases in which the need is directly obvious. It is
nevertheless a right which the merchants themselves must
recognize; since they claim it for themselves, they must
recognize it in those with whom they trade. They must find a
way by which it can (normally, at least) be established.

The need for protection of contract arises in the following
manner. Even the simplest exchange is a species of contract;
each of the parties is abandoning rights over the thing that he
sells, in order to acquire rights over the thing that he buys.
Now it will happen, very early on, that the things to be exchanged are not, or not all of them, physically present at the
moment when the agreement to exchange them is made.
Thus the bargain has three constituents which soon become
distinguishable; the making of the agreement, the delivery one
way, and the delivery the other. As soon as this distinction is
made, the agreement itself becomes no more than a promise
to deliver. Trading is trading in promises; but it is futile to
trade in promises unless there is some reasonable assurance
that the promises will be kept.

A promise may fail to be kept just by bad faith—by deliberate deceit; but even if there is no deceit, it may fail in

other ways. There may be misunderstanding between the parties on just what was promised; so that when delivery is made, though it is of what the seller had planned and expected to deliver, it is not what the buyer had planned and expected to receive. Again it may happen that by some unexpected event the seller is unable to fulfil his promise; he may die, or the goods he had planned to deliver may be destroyed, or may be stolen from him. Such possibilities (and there is an immense variety of them that can arise in different sorts of trading) can never be wholly excluded. Though contracts can be drawn up which provide for many of these eventualities, it will not be worth while, in the midst of active trading, to provide expressly for every such possibility in every bargain that is struck. Trading will thus be immensely facilitated—it is practically a necessary condition for continuous and active trading—if there is some general understanding of what is to happen if there prove to be obstacles to the performance of the contract, as it was originally understood by either party, or by both.

Between merchants and non-merchants it is by no means easy to build up that understanding; and this is a major reason why on the boundaries of the mercantile economy (as we shall be calling them) there is so often friction—friction which attends the whole story of mercantile development from its beginnings even right up to the present day. In dealings between merchants, of one merchant with another, it is in principle much easier. If the parties to an agreement are doing the same kind of business, there is reason to expect that it will be interpreted by both in the same sense and with the same overtones; they 'speak the same language'. But even in dealings between merchants there can be misunderstandings and there may be deceptions; and there will be contingencies for which no provision has been made. Disputes will therefore arise, and there must be means of settling them, in order that contracts should be reliable. Legal (or at least quasi-legal) institutions are therefore required.[1]

[1] I should like to acknowledge the debt which I owe to Professor Herbert Hart's *Concept of Law* (Oxford 1961) for clearing my mind on these matters.

Now it is to be expected that the customary, or command-customary, system, out of which the mercantile community is endeavouring to develop, will have its own means of settling disputes; but the characteristic features of that old legal system (though they survive in many ways into the legal systems of more modern times) are not such as to meet the needs of the market, certainly not such as to meet them at all easily. The old principles of settlement, in terms of customary rights and duties, are by no means such as are now required. It is the nature of the rights arising out of contract which now needs to be settled. There are some contracts (like the absurd contract which Shakespeare uses to parody the issue in *The Merchant of Venice*) which it will be obvious should be set aside; but there are many less extreme cases where what is to be done is by no means so obvious. The important thing, from the point of view of the smooth working of the mercantile economy, is that even on the more difficult matters clear decisions should be given. Then, though one contract may be invalidated, further contracts will not be invalidated; those who enter into contracts will be able to know what can be enforced and what can not. But these are not the kind of decision which comes at all easily from judges whose background is in customary law.

Both the protection of property and the protection of contract must be established, at least to some extent, if the mercantile economy is to flourish. They are not provided by the traditional society; but they can be provided, to what (up to a point) may be a sufficient extent, by the merchants themselves. They may join together, as we have seen, to protect their property from violence; they may establish rules among themselves for the verification of property rights; and they may police their contracts, even if the regular judges do not do what is needed, by including within the contracts provision for arbitration—arbitration by another merchant rather than a judge. This, however, can hardly be possible unless the mercantile community has already acquired some social linkage or articulation. A random collection of individuals will hardly have it; but one can understand that there are occasions on which, even at the start, it will be available. Merchants who are members of a particular ethnic or religious group, even of one that was not highly regarded among the peoples from whom they have been extruded (or have extruded themselves), may well have their own natural leaders; among those leaders, who are also merchants, the arbitrators who are required may be found. One thinks of the Jews, and perhaps of the Parsees; or indeed of any group of merchants, with the same origin, who find themselves operating in a foreign country.

On this basis much can be done, and there are other instances in which one must conclude that it has been done. I do not think that the legal systems of Eastern Asia, before the Western impact, ever accommodated themselves at all easily to the needs of the merchant.[1] Yet there is no doubt that in old China and in old Japan there were significant mercantile expansions. China had a great expansion of overseas trade (lasting, however, for a curiously short time) in the early days of the Ming dynasty (fifteenth century); while there was a great expansion of internal trade within Japan in the seventeenth century under the Tokugawa. We are informed[2] that the merchants of seventeenth-century Osaka were even able to proceed to the most sophisticated mercantile dealings, such as the establishment of futures markets. They must clearly have done this with little assistance from the political institutions of their country; they must have found a way by which they could police their contracts, to a sufficient extent, by arrangements which they made among themselves.

Thus it can be done; but a mercantile economy that is organized on this basis is inevitably confined. It does not have

[1] The drastic reform of their legal system which the Japanese were obliged to undertake, as part of the modernization which followed the Meiji revolution, is an indication of this.

[2] E. S. Crawcour, 'Development of a Credit System in 17th century Japan,' *Journal of Economic History*, Sept. 1961, p. 350.

This Osaka trade arose out of the transmission of rice revenue to the Shogun's capital at Yedo (modern Tokyo) from western and central Japan. It is thus an excellent example of one of the processes of market development which we have already noticed (above, p. 32).

the power of growth, of spreading itself continually into new
fields and new applications—a power which it does have in
abundance when more regular legal institutions can be used.
But for this it is not only necessary that the rulers (whoever
they are) should look upon mercantile transactions with some
degree of favour. Favour, but a somewhat unreliable favour,
is not infrequently forthcoming; since there are several ways,
as we shall see,[1] in which it is convenient for rulers to have
merchants among their subjects. What is also necessary is that
they, together with their judges and administrators, should
have a 'feel' for trade, so that they can give it the kind of help,
or rather recognition, that it needs. This is a difficult require-
ment to meet, but there is one condition in which it will be
met. It will be met if the rulers are themselves merchants or
are deeply involved in trade themselves.

How can that happen? It is not enough that there should
be a king who is employing traders to do pieces of trading for
him (as Pharaoh and Solomon will have done); at the stage
we have now reached, more than that is required. We must
postulate a community in which trade has been able to
acquire some social importance; the trade which rises most
easily into the requisite importance is external trade. But if
external trade is to gain this importance, the opportunities
which it offers must be large, relatively to internal opportunities; and it is easiest for that to happen in a community
that is rather small. The need is therefore for a small
community, with good opportunities for trading outside it;
but it must be an independent community, independent
enough to be able to mould its institutions to meet its own
needs. These are stringent conditions, but there is a well-
known case in which they are met. They are met in the City
State.

The fact that European civilization has passed through a
city-state phase is the principal key to the divergence between
the history of Europe and the history of Asia. The reason why
it has done so is mainly geographical. The city state of
Europe is a gift of the Mediterranean. In the technical con-

[1] Below, pp. 61ff.

ditions that have obtained through the greater part of recorded history, the Mediterranean has been outstanding as a highway of contact, between countries of widely different productive capacities; further, it is rich in pockets and crannies, islands, promontories, and valleys, which in the same conditions have been readily defensible. Asia has little to offer that is at all comparable. The Inland Sea of Japan is tiny in comparison with the Mediterranean (it is not even as large as the Aegean); the districts that surround it do not differ in natural resources as the Mediterranean countries do. As for the China sea itself, it was for long an obstacle to trade; so formidable an obstacle that its terrors are a main reason why the civilization of Japan was not swallowed up in that of China at the beginning of their history. The unbroken coastline of India offers few opportunities for trading along it. Perhaps the best hope, on the whole map of Asia, is the southeast corner (Indonesia and Indo-China). It is there most conceivable that a trading system, like that of the Mediterranean, could have grown up. Opportunities, however, were less and difficulties greater. It has indeed been a place where for many centuries there has been a good deal of maritime trading; but until the rise of Singapore, in very recent times, it has not been a place for city states.

One thinks mainly of the Greek city states; but the city state is a social phenomenon that is more general. It is not just a creation of the Greeks. Before the Greeks there were the Phoenicians (Tyre and Sidon and Carthage); contemporary with the Greek city states were the city states of the Etruscans. It is still more striking (and clearer evidence of the generality of the phenomenon) when we find the same story being repeated, at a much later epoch but on similar ground, with the city states of Mediaeval Italy and of the Italian Renaissance. It is the same story; much of what I shall be saying in the next chapter about the economics of the city-state phase will apply to both. It is however true that at this later period there had been technical developments (in particular the evolution of the sailing-ship[1]) which had deprived the Mediter-

[1] J. H. Parry, *The Age of Reconnaissance* (London 1963), Ch. 3.

4—T.E.H.

ranean of some of its predominance. City-state development could therefore extend into more northern waters. So we come to the Hansa towns of the North Sea and the Baltic, and to the city states (as they effectively were) of Germany and of the Low Countries.

Naturally we know much more about the economic structure of these later city states than we do about the Greeks. The primacy of the trading interest in Amalfi and Pisa, Genoa and Venice is unmistakable. It is significant that of the ten 'Major Arts' (or guilds) which largely took over the government of Florence in the thirteenth century, seven were in export trades. The position in the Greek city states is much more obscure. The period of their trading expansion is very early; it is usually dated at 750–550 B.C. From that early period we have little that is relevant in the way of literary sources, though archaeology makes the fact of the expansion incontestable.[1] It is generally held by ancient historians[2] that the ruling classes of the Greek city states at this date were landowners, not merchants; it may, however, be respectfully suggested that when trade is as active as it appears to have been, even a landowning class is likely to have been engaged in trade to an extent which is sufficient for the trade orientation.[3] Some, perhaps many, of the traded goods will surely

[1] N. G. L. Hammond, *History of Greece* (Oxford 1959), esp. pp. 130–31.

[2] As, for instance, by Prof. A. Andrewes, *The Greeks* (London 1967), Chs. 6–7.

[3] There is even a passage in Homer in which we seem to see just this happening. In the first appearance of Athene to Telemachus (*Odyssey* i. 180–4), she takes on the disguise of a certain Mentes, who describes himself as 'ruling over' a maritime people (the Taphians), but who is on a voyage with the object of trading a cargo of iron for one of copper. He is the son of a warrior, and had been a friend of Odysseus; thus there is plenty of evidence (not just the word ἀνάσσω) that he is to be taken as belonging to the ruling class. Yet he is engaged in trade.

Mentes, of course, is a fictitious character, a fiction within a fiction. But this strengthens my contention. The story he tells would be pointless unless it was plausible, unless it was the kind of thing which the poet's hearers would accept without saying to themselves 'how odd'.

There are of course plenty of passages, in ancient as well as in more modern writers, in which the social status of the merchant is regarded as low, at best 'middle class'. On the view of his evolution that has been taken here, according to which even the greater merchants have developed from the class of lord's servants, that is not at all surprising.

have been farm products; the poet's picture of the Grecian coaster

> Freighted with amber grapes and Chian wine
> Green bursting figs and tunnies steeped in brine[1]

is surely acceptable, though he will have carried other things too. Why should we assume that such goods were always, or even normally, the personal possessions of the ship's master? They must have come from the farms or estates; if they were entrusted to the trader by the stewards of those estates, the estates themselves were engaged, if only indirectly, in trade. No more than that is needed.

Looking at what is common to all these examples, we shall hardly go wrong if we treat the 'typical' city state as a trading entity: a form of organization which in the history of the Western world, and now in consequence in the history of the whole world, is of central and critical importance.

[1] Arnold, 'The Scholar Gypsy'.

IV

CITY STATES AND COLONIES

WHEN the city state is considered as a political organization, it has a history (in which Ancient Greece and Mediaeval Italy are the outstanding episodes); and it has a theory, which has been a preoccupation of political philosophers, from Plato and Aristotle onwards. When it is considered as an economic organization, it has a corresponding history; and in that aspect also it is so distinctive a history that we might expect it to deserve something of a theory to correspond. I shall endeavour, in this chapter, to sketch out an economic theory of the city state, or system of city states, the system which we have identified as the First Phase of the Mercantile Economy. It will be a 'model', like other models that are used by economists to elucidate the working of economic institutions (the textbook model of the nineteenth-century Gold Standard is an obvious example). We do not suppose, when we use such a model, that it is describing what actually happens, or has happened, in any particular case. It is a 'representative' case, from which particular instances must be expected to diverge, for particular reasons. But when we find a deviation from the model, the model will tell us to ask 'Why?' If it is a good model, the 'why?' (sometimes at least) will be an interesting question.

The core of the city state, regarded as a trading entity, is a body of specialized traders engaged in external trade. They are trading, in part, with merchants in other city states; the whole body of traders, in mercantile relations with one another, over the whole group of city states, constitutes the Mercantile Economy, the system of people and relations between people which we are to study. Even in this wide sense the Mercantile Economy is still an Open Economy, which exists by trading with people outside it. We reckon these outside people as non-merchants; for though they trade with the merchants they are not specialized traders. The Mercantile Economy, at this stage, is thus to be regarded as a system of trading centres, trading with one another but ultimately dependent upon trade with the outside world.

Let us begin, in the regular tradition of model-builders, with a simple case, perhaps the simplest case. There are (say) two 'outside' areas, in one of which corn is scarce but oil is plentiful, while in the other it is the other way round. We need not, for the present, introduce money, for though the trade which we shall be analysing could be conducted in money terms, it is not necessary that it should be.[1] All that matters is that in the one area oil can be sold at a high price in terms of corn, while in the other corn can be sold at a high price in terms of oil—that is to say, oil has a low price in terms of corn. It does not matter which we use as a standard of value; it is the same story in either. But it will make for clarity if we choose one of them and stick to it; let us take oil.

Then the merchant is making a profit (in terms of oil) by buying corn at a low price and selling it at a high price; and the trade is unlikely to get started unless, to begin with, it is a handsome profit. Nevertheless, since the corn producers are willing to sell their corn at the price which is paid to them, it would seem that they must be deriving *some* advantage from the bargain; for unless they derive some advantage from it, why should they enter into it? The price which is offered to them must be greater than their 'sticking price', the price at which they would just refuse to sell; at that price they would get no advantage, at any higher price they must get some advantage. In this sense there must be an advantage to the sellers of corn (the buyers of oil); and there must be a similar advantage to the buyers of corn (the sellers of oil) for just the same reason. Thus there is a profit to the merchants, and a gain (a different kind of gain, but no less real) to each of the parties

[1] I shall come to money in Chapter V.

with whom they trade.[1] So long as the trade is voluntary, it must confer an All-round Advantage.

This is a valid and important principle; much of what follows will depend upon it. Nevertheless it requires qualification (or interpretation) which, in the further applications which we shall make of it, I shall try to be careful to make. Already, in our simple corn–oil trade (which is no more than an example), there is a form of the qualification which should not be omitted. It may be (it is quite consistent with the story I have been telling that it should be) that the corn is not purchased by the merchants directly from corn producers, but from lords in the corn country, who have received it as revenue. If that is so, though it remains clear that the trade is to the advantage of these lords (since they do not have to engage in it unless it is to their advantage), it by no means necessarily follows that it is to the advantage of their subjects. It can be that it is to their disadvantage. It can be that the new way of using his corn revenue, which is presented by the trade, stimulates a ruler to extort a larger corn revenue from his subjects than he had been content with previously. The gain which he gets from the trade is thereby increased; but this extra gain is at the expense of his subjects.[2] This is one way (as we shall see, it is not the only way) in which the growth of trade may have *distributional* effects that are not in accordance with the principle of All-round Advantage.

Let us return to the merchants themselves. They have bought their corn at a low price (in terms of oil) and sold it at a high price; a substantial profit remains, which we reckon as so much oil, since we are taking oil as our standard of value; but there is, of course, no reason why it should not be taken partly in oil and partly in corn. They may consume this profit directly or they may use it for further exchanges with other non-merchants, who provide them with other goods for them to consume. But there is another thing they may do with

[1] In technical language, the latter gain is a consumer's surplus.

[2] An even more sinister example of what is at bottom the same phenomenon is to be found in the way the expansion of a slave trade encourages slave raiding, as we know that it did among the tribal communities of West Africa in the seventeenth and eighteenth centuries.

it. We do not have to make any special assumption about 'capitalist mentality' in order to conclude that some of them will use a part of their profit in this other way, that is to say, to expand their trade. 100 units of oil, sold for corn and then re-sold for oil, have become 120 units. The merchant must repeat the operation, if he is to continue his business; but now he has more than 100 units of oil with which to repeat it. For this reason alone it is to be expected that trade will grow. A less profitable trade might have been less inclined to grow; but a profitable trade will grow, simply by the reinvestment of profits.

It would nevertheless be expected, by a straightforward application of conventional economic reasoning, that the growth of the trade would narrow the profit. In order to extract a greater volume of corn from the corn producers, the merchants would find themselves having to offer them a better price; and in order to sell more at the other end, they would have to take a lower price; so the gap between the selling and buying price would diminish, which is to say that the profit margin would diminish. The gain from trade, which at the first round accrued very largely to the merchants, would thus be transferred to the non-merchants—how much of it going to the corn-producers and how much to the oil-producers depending on which it was that had a demand that was more easily glutted. But since relatively less of it would be going to the merchants, their profits would fall, relatively to the volume of trade. The rate at which their capital could be increased would therefore be diminished, and the rate at which trade could expand would therefore be slowed up.

Doubtless this argument has some validity; the tendency to which it draws attention must be one of the forces at work. We have to invoke a 'tendency to diminishing returns' of this kind in order to explain trade diversification—the very characteristic endeavour of the merchant to look for new objects of trade and new channels of trade, the activity which makes him an innovator. A simple trade, such as the corn–oil trade between two areas with which we began, must surely have a limit beyond which it could not expand; there would be a decline in profitability as that limit was approached. But as the profitability of that trade declined, the merchants engaged in it would be looking for new ways of investing their capital. They would be seeking to open up new markets for the disposal of their 'corn' or of their 'oil', extending the corn–oil trade into other areas, or converting their stock (of one or of the other) into new commodities so that they developed new channels of trade. This is what it would be profitable for them to do; it is what we should expect to find them doing, if ways of doing it could be found. It must, however, be noticed that the opening up of new channels involves new contacts, the making of contracts with new sorts of people (merchants or non-merchants); and how are these new contracts to be enforced? The arbitration arrangements, which (as we have seen) it is possible for a group of merchants to make among themselves, depend upon their social cohesion; it is therefore not easy to extend them outside the group. Thus if it is necessary to rely upon such arrangements, there is an obstacle to diversification which may well be insuperable. It is here that the city-state form of organization shows its superiority. The possibility of having recourse to regular legal institutions within the individual city state makes it easier for new kinds of trade to be carried on securely, under existing arrangements, or by an adaptation of existing arrangements; and though the legal institutions of different city states may not be identical, they are likely to be similar, so that some security is provided, though it is less than the security provided for transactions between merchants who belong to the same city. This, I think, is one of the main reasons why the city-state form of organization is so important. It is particularly favourable to the growth of a diversified trade; so it provides a way round the first form of the 'diminishing returns' obstacle to trade expansion.

I say 'the first form', for there is a sense in which a diversified trade is only a combination of simple trades. They will encounter limits to their expansion; why should the combination of them not encounter a similar limit, in the end? It may well do so, in the end; but a diversified trade has expansionary possibilities on the way which may well enable that end to be long postponed.

It is, in the first place, by no means necessary that the first of the opportunities for trading to be opened up should be those which prove to be the most profitable; there may be more profitable opportunities from going further afield which will not be discovered until the nearer opportunities have been explored. (The point is the same as the classical misapplication of Ricardian rent theory; it is by no means the case that in the settlement of a new country the best land will be the first to be occupied. The poor land of Massachusetts was cultivated for generations before the Americans found their way to the Middle West.) The same holds here; for this reason alone there may be a phase of increasing profitability, before the 'tendency to diminishing returns' sets in, when trade can only be expanded at a diminished rate of profit.

And it is probable that there is another reason. In trade, as in industry, there are genuine 'increasing returns' tendencies. As the volume of trading increases, it can be better organized so that the costs of trading are reduced. If he can reduce his costs, trading may be as profitable to the merchant as before, even though the margin between buying and selling price is narrowed. The gain to the non-merchant, on one side or the other, is increased by the narrowing on the margin; but the profitability of the trade, and therefore the urge to its expansion, is nevertheless not diminished.

It is not so much that the individual merchant operates more easily on a larger scale (though there may sometimes be something in that) as that he benefits when he is part of a larger body. The economies in question are mainly what Marshall called 'external economies'. These, at the city-state phase, are rather clearly recognizable. There are some which arise from the expansion of the individual city state or trading centre; and there are some that arise from the multiplication of trading centres, from the growth (that is) of the Mercantile Economy as a whole.

The expansion of the trade of an individual city may take

place by the growth of existing enterprises; but it may also occur by increase in the number of enterprises, by increase in the number of merchants who are attached to it. That outsiders (such as the well-known 'metics' of ancient Athens) should wish to come in, to take advantage of the protection accorded to merchants, needs no explanation; what is remarkable is that there should have been a phase in which their competition is tolerated, or even welcomed, by those already established. This can only be explained by supposing that the expansion, which the newcomers make possible, is in fact at that stage to the general advantage.

If the newcomers were to do exactly the same business as was being done by established merchants, their competition would probably, at best, be harmless; as soon as there was even a temporary check to expansion, it would be a nuisance. But in fact they do not need to do just the same business; their best opportunities will be to fill gaps in the already existing structure. The former merchants (we may now suppose) will not all of them be doing just the same business; there will be things which they have not been able to avoid doing for themselves and which they will prefer to let the newcomers do for them. By the expansion in the number of merchants operating, the trading centre as a whole will benefit from specialization and division of labour; so a larger centre will be able to trade, up to a point, more effectively than a small one.

The benefits in question are not only direct reductions in cost; even more important, perhaps, are reductions in risk. Every trader is operating in an environment of which he has fair knowledge only as concerns those parts that are 'nearest' to him; he has much weaker knowledge of parts that may concern him intimately, though they are 'farther away'. It will always be to his advantage to find ways of diminishing the risks that come from his imperfect knowledge, either directly by increasing knowledge, or indirectly by devising safeguards so that the things which come up out of the darkness may (probably) hurt him less. The evolution of the institutions of the Mercantile Economy is largely a matter of finding ways of diminishing risks.

This applies, in the first place, to the legal and quasi-legal institutions which we were formerly discussing: institutions for the protection of property and contract. These, it is immediately evident, will function better if they are not on too small a scale. It similarly applies to the proliferation of agents and branches and 'correspondents'. It applies to the development of particular forms of contract, such as insurance and hedging; as the scale of the market increases, the opportunities for these will increase so that they become increasingly effective. It will apply, when there is sufficient growth, to arrangements that can only be made by multilateral contract: trading companies, for instance, through which capital and knowledge can be pooled. In the early city state some of these developments may lie far ahead; but rudimentary forms of them are likely to occur long before much notice is taken of them. It will always be the case that the larger the number of traders who are in contact with one another, the easier it will be to acquire information; even more important, the easier it will be to shift risks—risks which arise for the single trader out of his own ignorance—on to the shoulders of those who in this respect are less ignorant, or who can find it worth their while to become so.

Such developments are clearly important within the individual trading centre; but they are also important as between trading centres, so that they play a part in the growth of the Mercantile Economy as a whole—the other kind of expansion which I was distinguishing. The mere fact that one trading centre has a different geographical location from another gives it some 'comparative advantage' in the collection of information; by trading between centres these advantages can be utilized and risks on both sides can be reduced. This applies, at any given moment, to trade between existing centres; but it also applies, very strongly, to the formation of new centres—*colonies*. The trading centre is dependent upon external trade; the Mercantile Economy as a whole, as I have repeatedly emphasized, is dependent upon trade with peoples outside it. There is a strong incentive to reduce the risks of that trade, by establishing trading-posts upon the foreign territory, which can hold stocks of goods, and can keep a watch upon the needs and inclinations of the customer or supplier. Even great mercantile expansion has been accompanied by some form of colonization. The Phoenicians spread their colonies round the Mediterranean; the Greeks round the Mediterranean and the Black Sea; the Mediaeval Italians (under the cover of the Crusades) spread their colonies, what were economically their colonies, round the north shore of the Mediterranean, from Acre and Rhodes, to Pera and Galata, to Barcelona; the trading states of Western Europe, in the sixteenth and seventeenth centuries, spread their colonies all round the world. It is hard to believe that it is not the same story, in some essential respects, in each case.

One must, however, make some distinctions. Not all colonies are mercantile; and not all mercantile colonies, even in their origin, are trading posts. There is a connection between mercantile expansion and colonization, but it works in more than one way.

From one aspect, colonization is just migration. Simple migration of a part of a community, from one area to another, could occur (for instance under population pressure) even under the *customary* conditions with which we started; it could occur, and has doubtless occurred many times over, in Africa, in Asia, and in the early history of Europe, without being due to trade or giving rise to trade. But there are several ways in which trade facilitates migration. Sites for settlement may be explored by trade activity; means of transport may be supplied by trading vessels; the contact with the home base, which can be preserved by a trading connection, makes the difficult period that is inevitably encountered in the early years of a new settlement easier to get through.[1] Thus the connection between mercantile expansion and colonization may amount to no more than a reduction in the costs of migration. The motive for the migration may remain non-mercantile, being traceable to population pressure or to social pressures of some other sort.

[1] There is a lively account of these difficulties, with special attention to the economic difficulties, in Bacon's essay on *Plantations* (1625). He is drawing, no doubt, upon the experience of the early English settlements in North America.

Another reason for the connection, it must be recognized, is military. Colonies, like their 'parents', have to be defended; the sea-power which has gone with maritime trade, in all of my examples, makes their defence a possibility. Colonies of settlement are likely to need defence against former inhabitants who have been dispossessed, and also against rival colonizers, Trading-post colonies (with which we are here more closely concerned) may sometimes be set up by agreement with the 'natives'; but since these are, at any rate initially, outside the Mercantile Economy, long-term contracts with them cannot easily be made *firm*. Misunderstandings lead to disputes, and disputes to wars; wars that from the standpoint of the traders appear to be defensive, though they will doubtless look different when seen from the other side. When experience has shown that the establishment of trading posts is likely to have such military consequences, it may become usual to establish them by military expeditions. There will be an element of force in the establishment of trading colonies, as there is in the establishment of colonies of settlement. It is a condition for each that force should be available, in some form or other, to back them up.[1]

The fact that force has been used in the establishment of a trading colony does not imply that the colony, after its establishment, is an exception to the principle of All-round Advantage. If it is simply used as a base for trade, the trade should be to the advantage of both parties, the merchants themselves and the 'surrounding' peoples with whom they trade. To these peoples the trade offers new opportunities, and these must represent in some sense a gain. They do indeed have to learn to make use of their opportunities; in the process of learning they will make mistakes, mistakes that will be costly, often very costly. But we can recognize the mistakes, and their consequences, without

[1] It has, of course, not at all infrequently happened that merchants who do not have force (or much force) behind them are permitted to set up trading posts on foreign territory, with the consent and under the regulation of the government of that territory. Such 'concessions', however, are not colonies; it would be generally insisted that they are not colonies. They do nevertheless represent an important development which must be filled in.

denying that the main trend must be advantageous. It is easy to be sentimental, or romantic, about the beauties of primitive societies; but it remains true that when people are offered a genuine opportunity for economic growth (for that is what this is) they are generally glad to take it. There are many and many frictions on the way; but the attention which we must give to the frictions must not blind us to the general trend.

It must nevertheless be insisted that it is implied in this optimistic verdict that the colony is genuinely a trading-post, and is not used as a basis for penetration of other kinds. Force that is used to establish security of trading can, only too easily, be turned to other purposes. It may be used for conquest, the economic objective of which is revenue or tribute—or just plunder. Thus it was the Venetians, a trading people if ever there was one, who sacked and ransacked Constantinople in what was called the Fourth Crusade. And thus it was that the merchants of the British East India Company, finding Bengal at their feet after Clive's victories, turned from trade to rapacious exploitation—in those black decades before order was restored by the true establishment of the British Empire in India under Cornwallis.[1] These are evils that belong to the situation; it would be easy to find other examples, ancient and modern.

It would further be absurd to pretend that those who are dispossessed by colonies of settlement are likely, even in the very long run, to be benefited. It is indeed not quite inconceivable that they may be; the country may be such that there

[1] The crucial event, which symbolizes the decision of the British government to enforce control, returning the merchant-exploiters to their proper places, is the trial of Warren Hastings. It is clear that Burke made many mistakes in his presentation of the case against Hastings, who had himself taken some steps on the road to purification, so that he was unlucky in being chosen as the victim; yet the moral triumph (for such it surely was) remains among the brightest spots in British history. It could only have happened because the 'Nabobs' had come home and flaunted their wealth; but think how strange, and how far away (in those days of the sailing ship), were the 'Gentoos' (as Burke called them) who were the sufferers.

Hastings is still on trial. For a modern statement of the defence, see Penderel Moon, *Warren Hastings and British India* (London 1947). The prosecution has been revived by P. J. Marshall, 'The Personal Fortune of Warren Hastings', *Econ. Hist. Review*, Dec. 1964.

is room for all, so that the former inhabitants may reap, in the end, by trade with the settlers, at least an economic benefit. But 'Where is the Indian in Massachusetts now?' It is the (relatively) happy ending which is exceptional.

There remains a possibility—an extremely important possibility—of which we have not yet taken account. I have so far been contrasting the trading colony with the colony of settlement; and it is the fact that there are many cases of colonization that fit, fairly cleanly, into one or other of these two classes. But there remains the case of the colony which is a colony of settlement *because* it is a trading colony. Settlers may come in, or may be introduced, not simply in order to support themselves as cultivators, but in order that the things which they produce should be objects of trade. The place of settlement has obvious natural resources (agricultural or mineral); the previous inhabitants are too few to exploit those resources, or are refractory to the attempts of the traders to persuade them to produce the tradeable goods they might be producing; the answer (the obvious mercantile answer) is to bring labour in from elsewhere. The labour may be brought as a slave labour, or as wage-labour, to work on 'plantations'; but there is also the possibility that the immigrants come in as free farmers, attracted by the possibility of selling a part of their produce. These (all of these) are penetrations by the market into primary production; and that is a matter the general consideration of which I shall defer, for it belongs, in my scheme, to a later stage than that which I am considering in this chapter.[1] It deserved mention here, for its beginnings are early. Even a pure trading-post needed food; the simplest way of providing it (very usually) would be to bring farmers in to produce it on the spot. Local production, in a community that was already oriented towards trade, would easily grow, if the land were suitable, into production for export. This is indeed what seems to have happened with the very early (seventh to sixth centuries B.C.) export of wheat from the Greek colonies

[1] See Chapter VII below.

in Sicily.[1] City states, however, can rarely have had the population or the power to develop very far in this direction. The main part of the story of plantation colonization belongs to more modern times.

I must return to my 'model'. We have followed the Mercantile Economy, in its city-state form, through the expanding stage of its development. The individual business has grown through the reinvestment of profits; the city by the growth of the businesses within it, and by the influx of newcomers; the family of city states has grown by colonization. In the process of growth trade has been diversified, and has operated more successfully and efficiently by economies of scale. Competition has become more intense so that the margin between buying and selling price has fallen; but the more efficient organization can manage on a lower margin, so that profit on capital is not reduced, or not much reduced; the rate of expansion is not much impeded by pressure on profits. The advantage of the trade to the surrounding peoples is nevertheless increased by the narrowing of the margin—increased, that is, 'on the whole', for there will be exceptions. Some of these exceptions we have already noted: distributional effects within the countries opened up by trade, the pushing out of 'natives' by settlers, and plantation colonies. But in addition to these there is the general exception which is inherent in a process of expansion, an exception which is very familiar in the expansion of an exchange economy, though in a process of expansion, however organized, some form of it is likely to exist. It is entirely possible that in one phase there may be a scarcity of some particular thing which some particular people are able to supply, so that they get adjusted to producing it and do well by producing it; but a better source is discovered at a later stage, so that the advantage which had accrued to the first group at the first stage is subsequently diminished. In

[1] T. J. Dunbabin, *The Western Greeks*, Oxford 1948, (esp. Chs. 1 and 7) gives a graphic reconstruction of the stages in the economic evolution of the Greek colonies in Sicily and Italy: a reconstruction which to the economist is very acceptable indeed.

the case of the mercantile expansion, so far considered, it is by the opening up of new sources of supply, in new geographical areas, that the damage to the original producers would mainly occur; but it is just the same as that which happens in our day through technical discovery. It is still the case that the discovery of new oilfields is a threat to old 'high cost' producers; but now we have synthetic rubber similarly threatening natural rubber. The technical innovations of our day have aggravated the problems of depressed groups and depressed areas; but there is no reason why they should not have appeared, long ago, in consequence of a trade expansion which was purely geographical.[1]

It may be said that the losses, and wastes, which result from the opening up of sources of supply that in the end are not wanted, are consequences of 'imperfect foresight'. That is true, but it is not helpful, for the expansion itself is a matter of imperfect foresight; it is a process of finding out, and finding out implies mistakes. It is more to the point to emphasize that in all such shifts there are gains as well as losses. The gains and losses accrue to different people, so that we cannot easily set one against the other; yet there is a sense, which is recognizable when we look at the matter from a distance (as we may do when we are considering the Greek expansion)—but much less so when we are close up against it—in which the gains must be dominant. This is again, though on a larger scale, a distributional matter; the advantage 'on the whole' to the surrounding peoples still remains.

We should be careful to notice in just what it is that the advantage mainly consists. Gains and losses that result from price-changes (such as those just considered) would be measurable easily enough by our regular index-number technique, if we had the facts; but the gains which result from the availability of new commodities, which were previously not available at all, would be inclined to slip through. (This is the same kind of trouble as besets the modern national income

---

[1] It appears that the Sicilian wheat export, which was dominant at an early stage of the Greek expansion, was displaced, in the fifth century or even earlier, by the export of wheat from the coasts of the Black Sea (Dunbabin, op. cit.).

statistician when he seeks to allow for quality changes.) There can be little doubt that the main advantage which will accrue to those with whom our merchants are trading is a gain of precisely this kind. The extension of trade does not primarily imply more goods; its main function is not to increase the quantity of goods produced, but to reshuffle them so that they are made more useful. The variety of goods available is increased, with all the widening of life that that entails. This is a gain which 'quantitative economic history' which works with index-numbers of real income, is ill-fitted to measure, or even to describe.

All of these issues (some of them, it will be seen, quite live issues in contemporary economics) come into sight while we are considering the expansion of the Mercantile Economy— even if we are only considering that in its first form, when it is embodied in a system of city states. We have seen what the forces making for expansion are; but we have discovered, in the process of elucidating them, that there is a 'tendency to diminishing returns' on the other side. It is only by constant improvements in organization (which is what the expansion-ary forces are) that the tendency of the profit rate to fall can be offset. If the merchants fail to find new economies, so that they can trade more efficiently in existing markets, and if they fail to find new markets, they will find prices moving against them; or rather they will be in a position in which prices would move against them, if they attempted to expand the volume of trade. It is tempting to suppose that there must be a phase in which the one force is dominant, which must be followed by a phase in which the other is dominant—a phase of expansion followed by a phase of stagnation; but that does not need to happen. It may be so; but it may also happen that after a pause new opportunities are discovered, so that expansion is resumed. We must always be on our guard against too easy an identification of logical process with temporal sequence.

It is nevertheless inevitable that there will be pauses; and there may be stagnation. And here it must be emphasized that a cessation of expansion does not mean that the Mercantile Economy settles into an 'equilibrium'—the stationary competitive equilibrium beloved of theoretical economists. Each of the centres, at the time when the blockage comes, is still trying to expand its trade; but the competition of the others, which had formerly been tolerated, is now a danger. There had always been squabbles between the centres. There must have been, since though their legal systems may be similar, they do not have a common legal system. But it is at this point, when the growth of their trade begins to be constricted, that the formidable struggles between them are likely to break out. Such, we may reasonably suppose, was the long war between Venice and Genoa, that lasted for nearly forty years around 1400; and it is hard to avoid the suspicion that the Peloponnesian War, which began as a struggle between Athens and Corinth, is (in some of its aspects) another example.

The alternative is to behave as modern industrial giants behave when they find themselves similarly placed. Intermercantile warfare is destructive of profits, like cut-throat competition; why not seek a way out, by what after all is the normal mercantile method? Why not come to an agreement, tacit or explicit. to divide the market—to keep out of each other's way?

It will be easy to slip into such arrangements 'in restraint of competition', for they will not have been unknown—they will have had a part to play—even in the expansionary stage. I have emphasized the need, not least in that stage, to find ways of diminishing risks. If the merchant can achieve a greater security in one part of his trade, he may be enabled to take greater risks, to be more enterprising, in other parts. There will always be some departments of trade which at the moment seem less expansible; restrictive agreements, in these directions, may make it possible for opportunities in other directions to be exploited more easily. The change to a more restrictive atmosphere may therefore be gradual. As opportunities in general close in, or seem to close in, the fields in which it becomes tempting to protect oneself by agreements with one's competitors become more extensive. Gradually, in this way, the mercantile economy slips into custom; the merchant is accepting a place in a system of customary rights and duties. The 'social gravitation', to which we formerly found the command economy to be subject, is expressing itself in this way upon the mercantile economy also.

Yet this moment, when expansion is arrested, may from other points of view be a wonderful moment. Profits are still high, but it is a condition for their maintenance that they should not be invested in further expansion. Once that condition is accepted, there is wealth, and there is security. What can be better? The hurly-burly of the market-place has been brought into order. People have their places in society, places to which they must keep, but which are preserved for them, by protection against the intrusion of others. Through their guilds and suchlike associations, which are the means to this protection, they can explore new forms of human fellowship. It is almost a socialist Utopia; and it is the fact that many socialist Utopias have had elements of it.[1]

It has other blessings also. The vigour which marked the expansion may not immediately be lost; it must turn from trading innovation, but with security and wealth it can be turned to other fields. The expansion of trade had been an intellectual stimulus;[2] but when the point comes that it no longer absorbs the same energy, art can be pursued for art's sake, and learning for the sake of learning. It was at the end of her period of commercial expansion that Athens became

[1] Most explicitly, of course, the 'Guild Socialism', which flourished in England about 1910, and which had a permanent effect upon the work of G. D. H. Cole.

[2] The forms of this stimulus are often obscure, but the fact can hardly be doubted. Could Herodotus have written his history save by drawing on the knowledge of the East that had been accumulated by the traders? Could he have visited those countries, as we know he did, save by following in their footsteps? The very consciousness of Hellenism, as a unity amongst immense diversity, could hardly have taken so explicit and so fertile a form if it had not been set against the knowledge which the Greeks had already acquired, in their commercial expansion, of the Barbarians round about them.

Similar connections must exist in the Renaissance case, though they have not (to my knowledge) been much explored. One, which does not seem to have been remarked, may be mentioned. If one looks for the origin of the introduction of perspective, which revolutionized Florentine and then Venetian painting in the fifteenth century, there is a very plausible mercantile explanation. May not Brunelleschi have been looking at those *portolani*, those first scientific maps, in

the 'mother of arts'; it was after their commercial expansion was completed that Florence and Venice became the homes of the High Renaissance. These are the fruits for which we remember them; but autumn is the season when fruit comes.

These city states were built upon commerce; when their commercial vigour was departed they were in danger. Every economy is subject to changes and chances; when the ability to expand is lost, the ability to recover from disasters may go too. This is one of the reasons (though, as we shall see, it is not the only reason) why a Mercantile Economy may go into a decline.

which the Pisans, just before his date, had solved the problem of converting the picture of a coastline, as seen from a ship, into the orthogonal projection of that coastline on to a horizontal plane? His famous perspective drawing of the chess-board pattern on the pavement of the Piazza de' Signori (which we are told by Vasari was the beginning of perspective in painting) was exactly the converse to this. Consideration of the one problem would lead, very naturally, to the other.

V

MONEY, LAW, AND CREDIT

It is possible that a city state, or city-state system, may have (should we say may enjoy?) a long decline. Thus it was, I suppose, with the Hansa; and thus it was with Venice, which in the eighteenth century, when strength was departed, became no more than the city of Canaletto and Casanova.

> Where, eas'd of fleets, the Adriatic main
> Wafts the smooth eunuch and enamour'd swain[1]

After that, when the end comes, it is only a ghost that dies.

That is one thing that may happen, but there is another which is more important. Even while the city-state system has some life left in it, it may be brought to an end in a more violent manner. This could occur for external reasons, which from our point of view are mere chance; but there is also a reason which we should not reckon as chance, for it fits in. It is a consequence of the process I have been describing.

We have seen that the growth of the Mercantile Economy increases the wealth of those with whom it trades; by increasing their wealth, it increases their power. They may simply be made stronger by the sale of arms to them; city states, in competition with one another, will have no compunction about that; and there are less direct ways in which they are likely to learn devices and techniques which strengthen them. Much time may elapse before the strengthening is dangerous; for the first effect of the greater strengthening of the neighbouring monarchs may well be that they fight among themselves. Rebellions (fomented by the Greeks) kept the Persians

[1] Pope, *Dunciad* iv. 309 (written about 1740).

quiet; the Italian Renaissance was protected by the Hundred Years' War between France and England. But when the time comes for a military monarch, fortified by the reflection of the expansion of the Mercantile Economy, to have overcome his local enemies, the defence of the trading states, which had in the past been sufficient, is likely to fail. That is how it seems to work out in the cases I have taken as my principal examples. The Greeks become subjects (or subject-allies) of Macedonian monarchs; the Italian republics fall a prey to France and Spain.

That could be the end; and it may well be that in other (inevitably less famous) cases it has indeed been the end. If the invaders have learned no more than better armaments, they will merely destroy. The whole system, Mercantile Economy and semi-mercantilized fringe alike, will relapse into barbarism. The process which we have been analysing will be finished; it may begin again after an interval, but if so it will have to begin all over again.

This, however, is not inevitable; there may be a continuation. There will be, if the invaders are already sufficiently mercantilized for them to wish to retain some part of the mercantile institutions. They have been deriving an advantage from having merchants among their neighbours; if they recognize this advantage, they will desire that the association should continue. The King will prefer to have merchants among his subjects, even if they are not his servants, like the servants whom in the old days he had sent forth to trade. If he has reached this point at the time when he takes over, he will absorb the trading centres, but he will not destroy them.

This condition under which trading centres survive, under the protection—the somewhat fitful protection—of a State that is no more than semi-mercantilized, has been a standard form of economic organization over a great part of recorded history. I shall reckon it, in my theoretical structure, as a Second Phase of mercantile development; the city-state system (together with the economically similar but less potent system which merchants could construct for themselves when political conditions were less favourable[1]) being the First. It

---

[1] Above, pp. 36–7

will appear, when our structure is completed, as a Middle Phase, which will deserve that name, though it is represented in the record by conditions which start before, and continue after, what are commonly called the Middle Ages. The passage from First Phase to Middle Phase, and from Middle Phase to the Modern which we shall subsequently identify, is sufficiently recognizable, and sufficiently general, for a classification of this sort to be useful as a framework.

It was characteristic of the First Phase (in either of its forms) that mercantile communities were being built up in an environment which was substantially (or at least relatively) non-mercantile. The line between the Mercantile Economy and its environment was rather sharp. In the Middle Phase, on the contrary, that barrier is largely down; so the formerly non-mercantile environment is open, in a variety of ways, to penetration by the market. The story of the Middle Phase, as such, is the story of that penetration.

I shall be considering it, in this chapter and in the three which follow, under a number of heads. The 'penetration' is of many different kinds, so a division by topic is clearly necessary. It must nevertheless be admitted that it has its inconveniences.

It was possible, while we were considering the pure theory of commercial development (for that was in fact my subject in the preceding chapter) to concentrate upon elements that are common to different expansions; thus I could run my leading examples, the Greek expansion and the Mediaeval Italian expansion, in double harness. In the Phase to which we have now come, that will hardly work. There are Middle Phase characteristics to be detected in the sequel to the Greek expansion, and in the sequel to the Renaissance; but a comparative study of these sequels, considered in general, would not get us very far. There are 'penetrations' in each case; but some of the penetrations, in each case, are more successful than others. If we consider it generally, the Middle Phase which followed upon the Greek expansion must be held to have petered out; to have been followed, in Western Europe, by absolute decline, and even in the East (among the Arabs and

Byzantines) by arrested development.[1] It was this which made room for the fresh start. Nevertheless, as we shall see (and as it is not surprising to find), there are particular topics on which there is more continuity; so when we are looking at them, it will be the same Middle Phase that seems to run throughout. This is difficult; but by taking topics separately it will be made easier.

The first of the topics which I shall take—the first of the kinds of penetration which I shall examine—is the use of money. The Mercantile Economy itself, almost from the start, perhaps from the very start, has been money-using. I did not emphasize that aspect in my first description of it, since I wanted to go, in the usual economist's manner, 'behind the veil of money'. It was nevertheless a serious omission, which must be remedied before going further.

Money, for the greater part of recorded history, has meant coinage; pieces of metal with the 'image and superscription' of some ruler stamped upon them. Money has thus appeared to be a creation of the State; and it is unquestionably a fact that throughout all those ages the relation between the State system and the Money system has been very close. It is nevertheless quite clear that money did not begin as a State creation. There was money before there was coinage. In its origin, money was a creation of the Mercantile Economy; though it was the first of the creations of the Mercantile Economy which governments (even quite non-mercantile governments) learned to take over.[2]

[1] I am not unaware of the mercantile activity which persisted in the East (as described, for instance, in the article by A. E. Lieber, 'Eastern Business Practices and Mediaeval European Commerce', *Econ. Hist. Review*, August 1968, and by C. G. F. Simkin, *The Traditional Trade of Asia*, Oxford 1968). I think nevertheless that in terms of my analysis, the above statement is broadly true.

[2] It was perceived, on purely theoretical grounds, that this must have been so, by the Austrian economist Carl Menger; see his paper on the 'Origin of Money', published in English in the *Economic Journal* in 1891. (This is a paper which deserves to be regarded as one of the classics of monetary theory. It is a clear statement of Menger's doctrine, already adumbrated in his *Grundsätze*, that goods differ, not only in their direct utility, but also in their 'saleability', money being just the extreme case of perfect saleability. This is a very good principle from which a modern theory of money might start). What Menger perceived theoretically has been abundantly verified by the archaeologists.

One can see it appearing, quite naturally, in the evolution
of the market. Remember our middleman, in the village
market; the middleman who is becoming a stockholder, a
holder of goods which he intends to pass on. What goods
should he hold? Primarily, no doubt, the goods in which he is
a specialist, goods which he expects to be able to dispose of,
because people know that he is the kind of person who would
have such goods. But there is another kind of good which it
will also be useful for him to hold, goods in which he is not a
specialist, but which are so generally traded that it will be
easy to dispose of them to almost anyone. So he can use them,
when he needs to do so, to get new stock of his special goods.
Traders with different specialisms will naturally come to use
the same goods as 'generalisms'; because a good is a better
'generalism' the more traders there are who make use of it in
that way. A good which is easily storable, easily hidden, and
rather undamageable, is obviously a good which is specially
convenient for that purpose. So it comes about that gold and
silver displace other goods which might be used as 'generalisms'; it is a concentration which comes about by the natural
operation of market forces.

This, however, is the 'store of value' function of money; it
is rather probable that it was this function that the precious
metals first performed. Having once acquired this function,
they could proceed to become 'standards of value' and 'means
of payment'—functions that had previously been performed
in other ways that were less convenient. The need for a
standard of value must often have arisen, even in pure barter
transactions. Even though A has a thing that B wants, and
B has a thing that A wants, they may be unable to trade; for
though A would accept B's thing in exchange for his, B would
not accept A's as an adequate exchange for his, though he
would accept it in part payment. A's offer must therefore be
'made up' in some way, if the bargain is to be completed. It
may be made up by odds and ends of miscellaneous goods[1]

---

[1] I have read somewhere (but I am afraid I cannot place it) of a transaction
between two monasteries, in the Early Middle Ages (probably tenth century
by which two pieces of land were to be exchanged for one another. The estates

when a money payment is impossible. But it will be difficult to achieve such a complex bargain unless the parties have some means of valuing the things that are to pass—valuing them, that is, in terms of a common standard. It is not necessary, for this purpose, that the standard should be one of the things that enter into this particular bargain; it is only necessary that it should be something that is generally traded. When cattle are used as 'money', as has clearly been the practice in some early markets, it is this function of money which they must mainly be expected to perform.

Cattle are an inconvenient money, not only because they are only available in rather large units,[1] but because they are by no means of uniform quality. Now the precious metals, at the time when they first acquired a monetary use, though they were rather better, were not so very much better. To divide a piece of metal into regular fractional parts is quite a skilled job; until the art of metal-working had made considerable progress, metal of standard composition was not available. It was at the point when this barrier was overcome that the precious metals triumphed. Even previously they had had some monetary use, but they could not develop the potentiality that they possessed until they could be made *standard*.

It is at this point (as we can understand, and as the record verifies) that the State comes in. But just how does it come in? By providing a standard of quality and weight, the Mint is undoubtedly providing a service; but what is the motive for undertaking it? One can imagine the commercially minded city state setting it up as a (profitable) public service; that will happen in time, but it is not easy to see that coinage can have started in that way. Why should non-mercantile governments take so readily to coinage, as all the evidence is that they did? It seems to me that there is another, more convincing, explanation of the beginning.

were recognized to be of unequal value; but since no money was available to make up the difference, it had to be made up with a mixed bag of manuscripts and relics. It is hardly conceivable that a bargain of this kind could be made without something that was serving as a standard of value.

[1] One remembers the old man on a mission station who, when asked why he had never married, said he had never seen a woman who was worth one cow.

One can get a hint from what happens with another, more sophisticated, form of money—the bill of exchange. When a merchant passes on a bill, he writes his name upon it, thus guaranteeing it; without the guarantee it would not be received. When Croesus, King of Lydia, minted coins[1] was he not doing much the same thing? He was giving the money a guarantee, which made it more acceptable.[2] There was an advantage to him in doing this, since he could then more easily use it to get the goods he required, or might require, from the merchants who were his neighbours. It may indeed have been the merchants who, in the first instance, insisted upon some guarantee.

It may however be asked: 'If this is the case, should we not expect that merchants, as well as kings, would be stamping their 'coins'? It would not be surprising if some of them sometimes did.[3] But clearly it was the King's stamp which won out, and won out rather easily. The reason must surely be that it had a wider acceptability. A merchant's stamp might be accepted in Miletus, where he was known; but it would be much less acceptable in the hinterland, in Lydia.

[1] The first gold and silver coins are in fact attributed to Croesus (about 550 B.C.) Coins made of 'electrum' (mixed gold and silver, and therefore presumably less 'standard') go back to a date perhaps 100 years earlier. (See the chapter on 'The Origin of Coinage', *Cambridge Ancient History*, vol. 4, Ch. 5.)

[2] It would clearly be implied in the guarantee that the coinage would be receivable by the government itself, in the payment of taxes that were due to it; one of the supports for the currency would be its acceptability to the government that issued it. Stress has been laid upon this point by Mr. C. M. Kraay, in his paper 'Hoards, small change, and the origin of coinage', *Journal of Hellenic Studies*, 1964, which I am grateful to him for bringing to my attention. As he shows, it is a plausible explanation of the fact, to which the archaeological evidence points, that many of the early coinages had circulations which were confined to rather limited areas. Nevertheless, since the coinage must have been *issued* in the first place by the government, and since there is no reason to suppose that those receiving it would have had tax-obligations which were related to their receipts; and since the metallic content of the coins was evidently regarded as a matter of great importance; I cannot see that this acceptability by the State can have been more than one of the elements in the guarantee. Is it not possible that the localization of circulation may also be partly explicable by the facility of enforcement of contracts in a *recognized* money—what was to grow into the principle of *legal tender*?

[3] There may indeed be some evidence that they did (Cambridge Ancient History, Vol. 4, p. 127).

The King's stamp would be acceptable in his kingdom, and in the trading city. At the next step, of course, the governments of the trading cities would be following his example.

Coins being very durable, many have survived, so that the process of the diffusion of coinage can be followed out. There is little doubt that these Lydian and Ionian coins were in fact the beginning; but from that centre there was a rapid spread of coinage over the Greek world. These first coins were rather large coins, which must have been very valuable—confirming our impression that early metallic money must have been mainly a store of value. But during the fifth century smaller coins begin to be struck, so that there is a presumption that coins were being used more generally as a means of payment; later (about 400) there are bronze coins, unquestionably token coins, pure means of payment, which must have circulated at values in excess of their intrinsic values. Only when that point had been reached could Greece be reckoned to have become something like a fully monetized economy.

Coinage had meanwhile been spreading outside. After the kingdom of Croesus had been conquered by the Persians, the Persian governors of Lydia continued to mint coins; when the Persian empire was reorganized by Darius (521–486) he took over their coinage. Persian coinage was imitated in India; but the main development of coinage in India comes when India is exposed to the direct influence of Greece, during and after the invasion of India by Alexander (325). There was a corresponding expansion in the other direction. Even in the fifth century (or earlier) coinage was spreading into the Balkans; there are Roman (and Carthaginian) coins from the beginning of the third century; the (then) Celtic chieftains of central and western Europe begin to mint their coins more or less at the same time. It had all spread from the Greek (or Aegean) base. It was a permanent spread. Over most of Europe, and of nearer Asia, throughout all later vicissitudes, the use of money (chiefly, until lately, in the form of coinage) has never been altogether abandoned. Mercantile transactions have declined, and the use of money has (naturally) declined with them; but wherever commerce has been active, it has regularly been money-using.[1]

This is the first of the economic legacies of the Greek city-state system; it is one main reason why it was that in the 'Middle Phase' that followed the Mercantile Economy was kept in being. Though the use of the King's money had come about through market forces, it was so clearly an advantage to him that it should be used that he would not abandon it. He had a direct profit from minting (a profit which became more considerable whenever token coinage was acceptable); but the indirect advantage that accrued was surely more important. If he could get his revenue in the form of money (and he would soon be seeking to do that, so far as he could), he would be able to spend it, through the channels of trade, so as to get a flow of real goods, that had greater variety, and therefore greater 'utility', than he could get directly from taxation paid in kind. He would then become dependent upon trading, upon trading with those who were his political subjects. He could not abandon the Mercantile Economy altogether.

The second of the economic legacies (still of the Greek city states) is in the legal field.

I have explained that the legal institutions of the non-mercantile economy, which are on the whole the institutions that a conqueror might be expected to bring with him, are by no means suitable to the needs of the merchant. If the merchant is obliged to make use of such unsuitable institutions, his development will be hampered, as we have seen that it was hampered, to a considerable extent, in traditional China and

---

[1] The only great exception to this rule of Greek ancestry is the (historical) monetary system of China. This developed (curiously enough) at much the same period, but its character is so strikingly different that it must be independent. It seems clear that it was not, in its beginnings, based upon the precious metals; thus it is probable that it did not pass through a stage in which the 'store of value' function was pre-eminent. Chinese money passed straight into being a means of payment; thus it was that the Chinese were more receptive to paper money than the Westerners; it was not only their early invention of printing which made them adopt it earlier. (On the history of paper money in China, see G. Tulloch in *Econ. Hist. Review*, 1956.)

perhaps Japan. It might very well have happened that a constriction of that sort would have occurred in Europe also. Even though the King had been willing to make use of the merchants, he would not have understood their wants (nor would his judges and administrators have done so). They would have been driven back, in the way I previously explained, to make their own arrangements. They would therefore have been deprived of the advantage of making use of a regular legal system, being shut up within the confines of such arrangements as they could make for themselves.

This did not happen, or on the whole did not happen. The danger was avoided—because of what, within the framework of ideas that I am presenting, can only be regarded as a fortunate accident. After Greece came Rome.

The trading centres of the ancient Mediterranean were indeed absorbed into an empire; but the empire which finally absorbed them, and which retained its dominion for several centuries, was not an empire that was made by a military despot. It was an empire that was made by a city state, not (in its origin) a mercantile city state, but a city state all the same. In its origin, the Roman republic was a command-customary economy; but the Romans had early shown an exceptional skill in resolving the opposition between command and custom. To quite an exceptional extent, they were constitutionalists; because they were constitutionalists, they had legal ideas to which mercantile notions of property and contract were not altogether foreign. They were law-makers; within the law that they created they could—in the end—find a place for mercantile law.

The beginning, of course, was very different. In its origin (so far as that can be traced) Roman law is a matter of the determination of the rights, primarily rights against one another, of the persons (and families) in a quite restricted ruling class.[1] The principal property of this class was landed property; the rights of an owner of such property against his neighbours, and the way in which it should pass on his decease,

[1] I have been greatly helped in the composition of these (very tentative) paragraphs by the work of Mr. J. R. Crook, *Law and Life in Rome* (London 1967).

are typical of the questions which came up for settlement at this first round. Only with the expansion of the Roman state —and particularly after that extraordinary revolution (about 200 B.C.) when, in the course of a single lifetime, Rome was transmuted from a central Italian republic into the mistress of the Mediterranean world—did it become necessary to give these legal conceptions a wider coverage. A sharp line was still drawn between insiders (Roman citizens) and outsiders (peregrini). Outsiders (including the people of the Greek cities that were now dominated) were allowed to keep their own laws for their own purposes; but an accommodation between their arrangements and those of the Romans had to be found. It might well have been that whenever there was a clash, the masters would just have used their superior strength; and for a while, immediately after the conquest, that is largely what happened. But then, at the next step, Roman legality triumphed. Gradually the conquered were given Roman citizenship; and even before that, the rights which the Romans had established against one another were extended into rights that operated in dealings with outsiders also. Thus it was possible for the mercantile law, which the Greeks had already established[1] to penetrate into Roman law. Many of the Romans themselves, at this point, were becoming merchants; they had a need for it, and were ready to receive it.

There is a close relation between this legal development and the monetary development that I was formerly describing. For one of the most striking things about Roman law, in its 'classical' period (probably to be reckoned as the great age of the Empire, from Augustus to the Severi, roughly the first two centuries A.D.) is its extreme dependence upon valuations in terms of money and upon money payments. Disputes are settled by money payments; wrongs are righted (so far as law can right them) by money compensation. If we reckon this money penetration (as I think we should) as a form of mercantilization, the 'classical' Roman law is mercantilized

---

[1] Much less is known of Greek than of Roman law. Greek private law, in the Athenian version, is however being reconstructed in the work of Mr. A. R. W. Harrison, *The Law of Athens* (Oxford 1968).

to an extent which goes far beyond the content of its mercantile law in the strict sense.

Money and law (the law of the merchant) are in fact the two great economic legacies of the 'ancient world'.[1] They are gains that have lasted. Though the Roman Empire fell, and there was a relapse (over most of western Europe at least) into a command-customary economy of a much cruder sort, these things lived on, diminished but surviving. The money economy contracted, but did not wholly disappear. The Roman lawbooks remained, neglected but discoverable. Thus when the countries that had been Roman (not all of them, but many of them) passed into a new city-state phase—that of the mediaeval republics which I have hitherto been using as a parallel—their story does not just repeat, for they had these advantages. There was part of the work that was needed that did not have to be done again. They began by being moneyusing; they did not have to find that out for themselves. When they came to need a mercantile law, they did not have to make that for themselves. Roman law, with the prestige of the remembered Empire behind it, was still available. There was much that remained to be done, but they did not have to start from scratch.

And so it was that when they came to pass into their Middle Phase, when they fell under the dominion of the Great Powers (not yet nation-states, but the ancestors of our nation-states) they did not simply bring with them the monetary system, and the legal system, which they had inherited from their predecessors; each had undergone at their hands a further evolution. They had a mercantile law, which had grown out of Roman law, yet was by now much more explicitly a 'law merchant' than it had been in the days of the Romans. Nevertheless it was reckoned as Roman law; its history gave it authority. It had many vicissitudes yet to face. It had to learn to live with new kinds of constitutionalism, such as that which English law had distilled from feudalism, by a process of give and take which is one of the most confusing expressions

---

[1] I am not, of course, including technological legacies. As throughout this book, I take *economic* in a narrower sense.

of the English genius.[1] Even into English law it succeeded, to some extent, in penetrating.[2] Over most of the rest of Western Europe the Roman law of the merchant still rules supreme.

To that part of the story I can only allude, merely indicating where it fits in. The development upon the other side must be given closer attention. For what happened at the Renaissance was much more than just an increase in the use of money. Money was changing its character, beginning to link up with credit and with finance. The Renaissance was a key time for financial development; but it is remarkable that this should have been so, since Renaissance financiers were confronted with an obstacle to which their Greek and Roman predecessors had not been exposed, or much less exposed.

In spite of the famous remark of Aristotle about the barrenness of money, the Greeks and Romans had no compunction about the taking of interest; but to Christians the taking of interest was usury, and usury was sin.[3] The theological origins of the usury doctrine need not concern us; for it is simply the reflection of an attitude which is very understandable in mundane terms. It is just another example of the clash, which we have so often encountered, between the viewpoints of the

---

[1] For a rather classical example of this muddling, see below, p. 75.

[2] The reception of the continental law merchant into English law is reckoned to have been begun by the great Lord Mansfield (Chief Justice 1756–88).

[3] The official Islamic attitude to usury is not significantly different from the official Christian; but it is unlikely that it should be traced to the Prophet himself. It is true that there are passages in the Koran that are directed against 'ribā' which has been interpreted to mean interest; but the contrast is between 'ribā' and almsgiving (a virtue which to the founder of a viable religion must always be of particular importance). Thus it is easier to read them as directed against a more general acquisitiveness, like the 'more blessed to give than to receive' of the Christian gospel.

(This 'liberal' interpretation is defended in an interesting paper 'Ribā and Interest', by Fazlur Rahman, published in *Islamic Studies,* the journal of the Central Institute of Islamic Research, Karachi, March 1964. I owe this reference to Dr. S. M. Stern.)

Some of the Prophet's views on economic matters (as befits one who was formerly a merchant) would qualify him for membership of the Montpélerin Society. When asked, in time of dearth, to fix a maximum price for corn, he replied: 'Only God can fix prices' (D. G. Margoliouth, *Life of Mohammed,* New York 1905, p. 465).

merchant and of the non-merchant; it was the viewpoint of the non-merchant which was crystallized, as it is perfectly intelligible that it should have been, in the official doctrine of the Church.

To the merchant, in any age, financial dealings are a natural extension of trade dealings; he finds himself passing, almost imperceptibly, from one to the other. Even before the invention of money, goods that were owned by one person must often have been entrusted to another, for him to trade with them on behalf of the owner; it will be remembered that we were unable to complete our picture of quite early trading without the introduction of such 'agency' arrangements.[1] After the invention of money, it will often be more convenient to replace such physical entrustings by a money loan. Why not?

To the non-merchant (including in that category the judges and administrators of the semi-mercantilized State) there is a reason why not. True enough that when a loan contract is made, it is like any other bargain, such as one of simple exchange. It will not be made, or will not be made voluntarily, unless it seems to each party that he has an advantage to be gained from making it. (An advantage, that is, relatively to the position he would be in if there were no such loan.) But after the loan is made, and before it is repaid, all that is left to be carried out is the one-sided payment by the debtor. And this is the point at which disputes arise, a point at which the debtor is likely to feel himself to be the aggrieved party. He is a 'debt-slave'; he is being made to pay a tax to someone who has no right to exact taxes from him. So he throws himself, if he can, upon the protection of the court.

He feels more bitterly (we can again understand) about the interest he is to pay on the loan than about repayment of the principal. But it is easy to see that if there is any doubt about repayment, there must be interest; for no one will voluntarily part with money, as a commercial transaction, in return for anything less than a 100 per cent probability of the principal being repaid. (Compensation for default risk is, of course, not the only reason for interest; but it is the important reason in

[1] See above, p. 41.

the present context.) The greater the risk of default, the higher
(other things being equal) will be the rate of interest charged.
Thus, if the courts are strict in enforcing loan contracts, the
risks of lending will be less and the rates of interest that are
charged will be lower; but if they are lax in enforcing them,
being generally inclined to side with the debtor, the reverse
will happen. If they both take the debtor's side about repayment, and in addition are hostile to interest, they will
shut up borrowing and lending altogether, except in so far as
it goes on in mysterious ways outside the law. This is indeed
what for centuries they very largely did; while philosophers
and theologians were inventing subtle justifications for their
behaviour.

There is, however, a quite simple commonsense explanation
of it. Suppose the court does take a firm line, and insists that
the debtor must pay; how is he to be made to pay? You can
confiscate his property, if he has any; but suppose he does not
have any, or not sufficient, or what he has is out of reach.
What is the further sanction? In Greek and Roman times there
was a further sanction—the debtor could be sold into slavery;
it is clear that in practice this sanction was very generally employed, and its availability is very probably the main reason
why in those days there was not the bar against interest that
there was in the Middle Ages. If that door is closed,[1] there is
no simple solution. Imprisonment for debt (though that has
been quite commonly employed) is a very poor solution, for
who is to pay for the support of the prisoner during his cap-
tivity? Why should the State pay? Why should the creditor
pay? It does not help him to get his money back. It is very
understandable that even when the sanction of imprisonment
is available, courts should have been unwilling to use it save
as a last resort. It is much better, they will say, not to get
involved.

There is, however, a further alternative open to the lender
or potential lender, not yet considered. He may demand
security for his loan.

There are two kinds of security which (legally, and I think

[1] For further discussion of slavery, see below, pp. 124–30.

economically also) it is important to distinguish. The first is the pledge or pawn. The debtor then deposits with the creditor an article of greater value than the debt, with the understanding that it is to be returned to him when he repays. If he does not repay, he loses the article.[1] This is very good security for the creditor, since he will actually gain if there is a straight default; and if there is any dispute about the repayment, it will be up to the debtor to take legal action against him. In any such action, as compared with the former case, the parties are much more on a level; it is relatively easy for the court to take a tough line.

The market for lending on these terms is, however, likely to be narrow; since it is only borrowers who have things to pawn who can borrow in this way. The market can be widened, since the things that are offered in security can be more various, if the other type of lending upon security is used.

This is the hypothec (as Roman law calls it); what English law has confusingly[2] come to call a *mortgage*. Here the article that is security for the loan does not pass into the hands of the creditor, but remains with the debtor, who can continue to make use of it, only committing himself not to sell it before he has repaid. Here again the creditor may gain if there is a default; but his position is weaker, for now it is left to him to have recourse to the law in order to gain possession—if there is any dispute, as it is extremely likely that there will be. And it is not so easy in this case, as in the case of the pawn, for the court to be tough; but it is considerably easier, on the whole, than in the case of the unsecured loan. It can therefore more easily happen that the courts will be strict about the foreclosure of mortgages, even when their attitude towards lending on other terms is not encouraging. If it is difficult to enforce

[1] Strictly speaking, the creditor will usually be required to sell the pawned article, and to recoup himself out of the sale price; but before it comes to that, it is very likely that the loan will have been prolonged, so that what is finally owing is much the same as what the article is held to be worth.

[2] A mortgage (a *dead* gage) was originally the name of the other kind of security, the pawn. Its transference to its present meaning is a characteristic piece of English legal topsy-turvy. The story is conveniently summarized in A. W. B. Simpson, *Introduction to the History of Land Law* (Oxford 1961), pp. 225–9.

foreclosure, default by the debtor remains a formidable risk; but if it is easy to enforce it, default may actually be an advantage to the creditor. One can conceive of a condition in which the making of loans on land mortgage may be a rather easy way by which financiers can get possession of landed estates. They will then be eager to lend upon mortgage, so that the rates of interest they will charge on such loans may be quite low.

I think one may say that lending upon security, in one or other of these forms, has for long ages been the normal form of lending by merchants to non-merchants; even today it remains a common type. From the legal standpoint, it is relatively unobjectionable; thus even in the days when the ban against lending at interest was supposed to be in force, loans such as these did not find it too hard to get by. (It did not take much ingenuity to put the contract into a form such that the interest element was rather inconspicuous.) The case is very different with the unsecured loan, a risky activity for the lender, so that it tends to be accompanied by high rates of interest, still called *usurious*; and a torment for the legislator and judge, since it expresses itself in free contracts, freely arrived at, which cannot nevertheless be enforced without oppression. Why not solve the problem (it must often have appeared) by enforcing the one kind but not the other?

Unfortunately this will not do. For there is another variety of lending without security, which is essential to the mercantile community, which is not usurious, yet is difficult to distinguish legally from usury. This is the lending that is practised within the society of merchants, based upon the credit of the borrower, his reputation for paying his debts; if credit is good enough, pledge or security is unnecessary. Interest rates, in the market for credit-worthy borrowers, are likely to be low—perhaps the lowest in the whole 'spectrum'. If they are the lowest, the usurious rates are the highest; thus it is tempting to try to distinguish between them by setting a maximum to the rate of interest which will be legally recognized. This is the way out which was very commonly adopted when the ban against interest was relaxed. It is nevertheless a crude device, for differential risk is not the only determinant of interest; there are others also. Even the market for credit-worthy borrowing will not work smoothly if interest is subject to a legal maximum at a low level—such as the traditional 5 per cent.

For the development of the mercantile economy, it is the 'inside' market—the market for (more or less) credit-worthy borrowers—which particularly matters. At the time when the mediaeval expansion began, courts of law were not in a frame of mind to give that market much help. So it was driven back on its own resources. It had to find its own ways, not depending too much on legal decisions, of bearing financial risks.

The variety of the devices which have in the end been discovered to do this is immense; they are the basis of the vast, and vastly differentiated, financial system of modern times. It happened, of course, in time that the legal system caught up with them and enveloped them; so that now it is through legal forms that they are operated, and in legally established institutions that they are embodied. Now, like money itself, they have in a sense become part of the State system; but, like money, they did not begin in that way. They began as an autonomous market development, outside the law. We might even say that they were a substitute for law.

The basic need, on which the whole of this financial development is based, is the need for widening the circle of credit-worthy borrowers. Any successful merchant is likely to have a few other merchants, whose business he knows, from long experience of dealing with them; so he will be willing to lend to them—to 'give credit' to them—for such sums as he can afford. But this is not enough; the need for credit, in an active mercantile economy, extends far beyond such narrow circles. How is direct knowledge to be extended, by making use of indirect knowledge? There are two main ways.

The first is surety or guarantee. The circle can be widened if those who are trusted by the prime lender stand guarantee for those with whom he has less direct contact, but they have closer contact. A sufficient example of this method is the acceptance of a bill of exchange. The acceptor, in effect, is selling his 'confidence'; if a price can be found at which he is willing to sell and the other to buy, the market is widened. This, it will be noticed, is a method that can easily grow up bit by bit; it involves no necessary specialization, nor would it be particularly troubled by the bar against interest. So it is naturally the method from which financial development starts.

A more powerful method is the development of financial intermediaries (or middlemen). Here the loan is made to the intermediary (one of those who are trusted by the prime lender) in order that he should re-lend to those whom he trusts. When a business has become specialized in such financial intermediation, it is already, in the broadest sense, a bank. Banking, however, depends upon interest, rather explicit interest, in a way that the guarantee method does not. It is by borrowing at a low rate of interest (or by the provision of services, that are equivalent to a low rate of interest) that the bank makes its profits. Thus the appearance of banking, as a regular activity, is an indication that the bar against interest, at least in appropriate fields, is breaking down. This began to happen, it should perhaps be emphasized, long before the Reformation;[1] in so far as the 'Protestant Ethic' had anything

[1] It would appear that the formative period of Florentine banking was the sixty or seventy years that centre on 1300—what we commonly think of, in other connections, as the Age of Dante. It is by no means surprising to find these developments at the height of the mediaeval 'boom'; nor is it surprising that these early banks should have been very *unsound*, over-anxious to accept deposits, and not yet conscious of the conditions under which alone it can be prudent to put such deposits to profitable use. The famous 'crash' of the Bardi and Peruzzi in 1342 was only the culmination of a series of crashes. Later Florentine bankers, such as the Medici, were more cautious, so that they maintained themselves longer. There is even a still surviving Italian bank, the Monte de' Paschi di Siena, which bears proudly on its doors 'founded 1472'.

It is notable, nevertheless, that it was not because of usury laws that the early bankers got into trouble. It was sinful to lend at interest (the sort of sin one confessed on one's deathbed), but it was a sin that was very generally committed. It was better for the interest element to be concealed; as is shown by Prof. de Roover (*The Medici Bank*, Harvard 1965, pp. 10–14), the combination of a loan with an exchange transaction was the commonest way of concealing it. But it is not to be supposed that the merchants themselves, or the lawyers who were concerned with mercantile transactions, were taken in by such devices. They were becoming very tolerant. There is evidence that by such people, in fourteenth-century Florence, only rates of interest in excess of 20 per cent were regarded as definitely usurious; 15–20 per cent has been described as a 'grey zone' (A. Sapori,

to do with it, it was practice that made the Ethic, not the other way round.

Neither of these methods would in fact be as powerful as they have proved to be, if it were not for the possibility of spreading risks, the so-called 'Law of Large Numbers' which is the basis of Insurance. We know that the mediaeval Italians were acquainted with insurance contracts; maritime insurance, insurance against the loss of a cargo in transit, was already possible in the fourteenth century.[1] To undertake a single insurance of this type—involving a small but significant chance of a large loss, with no more than a moderate gain in the other event to set against it—would be intolerably risky; but it must soon have been observed that by combining a number of such risks, if they were reasonably independent of one another, the risk could be greatly reduced. If this had not been perceived, insurance could not have developed, as we know it did. We cannot tell at what point it was observed that the same principle applied to banking. Lending can *on the whole* be safe (or reasonably safe) even if the individual loan is not safe, provided that the loan forms part of a group in which the proportion of bad debts can be relied upon not to rise too high. It is possible that the Renaissance bankers were not in a position to make much use of this principle; but (at least from the seventeenth century) it has been a stand-by for their successors. Though, in its application to banking, it has been often abused, it remains a main way—perhaps in the end the main way—by which the market has been widened. There is continuous development from these beginnings to the consumers' credit and hire-purchase of the twentieth century, through which what appears to be a sufficient degree of creditworthiness has been discovered even in the 'man in the street'.

In these later stages, it is not the banker only who is enabled to spread. Even the small property-owner ('investor' or

'L'interesse del denaro', in his *Studi di storia economica medievale*, Florence 1947, p. 111.)

[1] According to Yves Renouard (*Les hommes d'affaires italiens du moyen âge*, Paris 1949, pp. 103–8) it was the Genoese who did most to develop insurance.

'capitalist'), as soon as there is a market for securities (loans), can place a bit here and a bit here, reducing his risks by spreading his portfolio. It is because investors can be attracted, if they are able to invest in this manner, that it has become worth while to borrow by *issuing securities*, and to set up markets (stock exchanges) on which they can be traded.[1] And even this is not all.

The most extraordinary development, in all this sequence, has been the invention of the Limited Liability Company, by which businesses have become able to raise capital, promising investors a share in profits. This began as a means to a further widening of the market for capital, it being found that it was sometimes possible to raise capital on these terms, when further borrowing at fixed-interest was difficult, or impossible. Partnerships, and legal arrangements for partnerships, go back at least to the Romans; but a partner has usually been liable for all of the debts of a business in which he is engaged, so that it is imprudent for him to enter, as a partner, into a business which is out of scale with his individual wealth. If he were to invest, as a partner, in several businesses, he would not spread his risks; he would face intolerable risks. When his liability is limited, so that he cannot lose more from the failure of a particular business than he has invested in that business, it becomes to his advantage to spread his investments, even if he has invested on 'equity' terms. That is the way in which limited liability widens the market.

The consequences of this arrangement, which cannot operate (it will be noticed) without legal sanction, are far-reaching. We shall meet them, as we go on, in several contexts.[2] They are near to the heart of the transformation which has brought the Middle Phase of mercantile development to an end, and has ushered in its Modern Phase.

[1] There was trading in securities on the Amsterdam Bourse as early as 1630 (C. Wilson, *Anglo-Dutch Commerce and Finance*, pp. 13–14). Even by 1688 London was 'hardly as yet challenging the international supremacy of Amsterdam' (P. Dickson, *Financial Revolution in England*, p. 486).

[2] See below pp. 98, 162.

VI

THE FINANCES OF THE SOVEREIGN

I TURN, in this chapter, to another aspect of the penetration by the market of its formerly non-mercantile environment: the effects of the monetary and financial developments, which I have been outlining, upon the State itself.

If there is one thing about kings (it is the regular kings and emperors of the history books who are chiefly, in our Middle Phase, in question)—if there is one general thing about them which we seem to learn from the history books, it is that more often than not they were hard up. Of course it is only since they began to use money that they have been short of money; but since that time this does seem to have been their general condition. Through their lack of money they have been put to the most desperate straits; savage confiscations of the wealth of Jews and Templars, civil wars in England and revolutions in France; while at the other end of the world there is evidence that Chinese dynastic cycles have been due, in part at least, to the same cause.[1] Yet all this time, as we have seen, the State has been involved in the money supply; but that has not helped. What is the explanation?

An underlying cause, in my opinion, is a rather chronic deficiency of tax revenue, which is one of the distinguishing characteristics of the Middle Phase. There is now enough trade for the general wealth of the economy to be increased, well above the level of its agricultural base; and the expenditure of the sovereign, governed by the kinds of things he is expected to do, is likely to increase *pari passu*. Or we should rather say that it would increase *pari passu*, if he could find the

[1] Reischauer and Fairbank, op. cit. pp. 117–8.

money to finance it. But here comes his difficulty. The old sort of land tax, levied on the peasant or serf (which had been the mainstay of revenue in the pre-mercantile system), even if it is extended to become a poll tax on the whole population, inevitably fails to tap the wealth of those who are now much more able to pay. How is their wealth—the wealth of the merchant class—to be taxed?

An obvious way of tapping it is by simple taxes on trade, customs duties, and so on. These have, of course, been employed right from the start of the Middle Phase (and, very generally, by city states); they do, however, have their limitations. I am not so much thinking of the well-known economic defect that taxes on trade are obstacles to trade; that as well as the trade that continues, and pays the tax, there is trade that is prevented, thus imposing sheer loss without gain to the government. What is historically of greater importance is that duties on trade can only be collected cheaply and efficiently if there is a large volume of trade that passes, and can be relied on to pass, a few specified points at which tax will be paid. The opportunities for this depend on geography. The Kings of England were exceptionally well placed, in that a large volume of trade, large in relation to total national wealth, passed through a few ports; doubtless this advantage had much to do with the long-standing relative efficiency of English administration.[1] Consider, by contrast, the case of the Roman Empire. We now know[2] that the Empire had more external trade than used to be supposed; but it passed over vast and often ill-defined frontiers, and even at its greatest extent, it must have been tiny in relation to total resources.[3] If taxes on trade must be taxes on internal trade, they have to be levied at artificial frontiers, which are difficult to police; and the trade which they prevent is sheer loss to the country as a whole. Many of the states of continental Europe, until quite recent times, have been in this position.

[1] Dating, at the least, from the reign of Edward I.

[2] Sir Mortimer Wheeler, *Rome Beyond the Imperial Frontiers* (London 1955).

[3] The Byzantine recovery, in the eighth to eleventh centuries, was based upon a trade-route through the Bosphorus, where it could easily be taxed.

But what about direct taxes? An efficient income tax is indeed an answer. But it is only quite lately (and even now not everywhere) that the conditions for the imposition of an efficient income tax have begun to exist. There can be no income tax until there is a means (an accepted means) of ascertaining income; but income is an economic concept that is quite sophisticated.[1] Mercantile development can go very far without the merchant having any reason to establish, even for his own purposes, what his income is. Certainly he must calculate his profit on a particular venture—on a trading expedition, for instance—but he has no reason to attribute that profit to a particular annual period, as must be done for the purpose of an income tax. It is only by the accumulation of conventions (some of which economists think to be quite odd conventions) that an acceptable way of taxing such profits has been built up. Thus, it was hardly possible for income tax to get off the ground at all until there was a fairly large body of wealthy persons with incomes that were easy to assess: landlords living on contractual rents, officials living on contractual salaries, and so on. These, in the case of early income taxes, are the chief income-tax payers; while the profits of trade (as was the case in France until a quite recent date) still largely escape.

What makes the difference—this is one of the ways in which it makes such a difference—is the institution of the Limited Liability Company (or Corporation). If the liability of shareholders is limited, something must be done for the protection of creditors (otherwise the Company would be unable to borrow); one of the protections that is given them is the obligation, laid upon the Company, to abstain from paying dividends out of capital. This makes it necessary for the Company to determine, quite definitely, what its distributable profits are.[2] When they have been ascertained, initially for

[1] There is an extensive economic literature on the concept of income to which the present author has contributed (*Value and Capital*, Oxford 1946, Ch. 14). The 'income' on which tax is levied (changing in definition from time to time) does not have more than a very rough relation to the theoretical ideal.

[2] As long as the rate of tax remains low, it is generally not in the interest of the company itself to understate its profits. For by showing itself to be profitable

this other purpose, they become taxable. What is distributed is taxable, and so is the remainder of the distributable profit which is not distributed. But this is not a stage which was reached—anywhere—until the middle of the nineteenth century; I have explained that I regard it as a major sign that the Middle Phase is giving way to something different.

In the absence of an income tax, it was necessary to fall back on a property tax, using property as an index of wealth. This is in fact what was often done, at least from the time of the Romans. Modern economists are inclined to maintain that a property tax (or capital tax) is superior to an income tax, and it is true that an ideal capital tax does have some theoretical advantages; but the property tax that has existed in practice has (always, I think) fallen very far short of that ideal. For in order that there should be an effective property tax, property must be valued; this is quite a difficult operation. (Property values, for instance, do not obey the laws of arithmetic; the value of one piece of property A *plus* the value of another B, when A and B are sold separately, are not necessarily equal to the value of A + B when they are sold together.) Again, therefore, it is only the property that is held in the more easily valued forms that gets taxed; by holding property in more mysterious forms tax can be evaded. But further, since valuation is difficult, and expensive to carry out, it will not be repeated very often; so that the taxpayer will usually be paying on what his property was worth some time ago, not on what it is worth now.[1] This does not only mean that the tax base is 'eroded' if there is inflation. It is eroded by all

(whether or not the profits are distributed) it improves its credit. At modern rates of tax (even the 50 per cent which is becoming the accepted rate in a large number of countries) the position is indeed different. It is no longer in the interest of the Company itself to co-operate with the tax-collector, so that a heavy burden is laid upon administrators and accountants if they are to prevent avoidance. It may be too much to conclude from this that taxes on profits can only be collected efficiently if they are introduced at low levels and only raised rather gradually; but there is a good deal of evidence which points in that direction.

[1] A curious example of this lag, surviving into the modern world, is the rating system of the Irish republic. Why does the town of Cork have a local rate of more than 90s. in the £? Because the rate is based upon valuations that date from 1850.

sorts of changes and chances, which put up some values (so that there is property which ought to pay and escapes) and down other values (so that the taxpayer is unable to pay what is demanded of him and has to be let off). The history of taxation is full of examples of property taxes, which have just gone bad.

Thus there are several reasons, purely tax reasons, why it was often very difficult for Middle Phase governments, even on the average over a long period of years, to raise the revenue that they required. The 'tax-base' was narrow; collection was inefficient, and (just because it was inefficient, falling on those whose liability was easy to assess, and letting others escape) it was inequitable; and the inequity of the system was one of the reasons why the revenue was so inelastic. So long as taxes remained unchanged, the inequity could perhaps be borne; but whenever there was a change, it showed up. For the revenue system, it will be remembered, goes back to the pre-market economy; it is based upon the rights, the customary rights, of the ruler in that economy; if he tries to squeeze out more revenue, by raising tax rates, or by imposing new taxes, he is stretching his rights. He will then, in the popular view, be no legitimate sovereign but a 'tyrant'; so he will be in danger of arousing a Wat Tyler or a John Hampden—or a Boston Tea Party.

But the problem is not only one of a long-run tendency for expenditure to increase. The increase was not smooth and gradual; it proceeded by fits and starts. Inevitably there would be emergencies, of which wars were the most important, but not the only kind. What was the King to do about his 'extraordinary' expenditure?

The obvious answer, we would now say, would be to borrow. But how was he to borrow? Borrowing (for the duration of the emergency) implies repayment; and how was he to repay? He would still find himself, when the emergency was over, in a position where his tax revenue was no more than sufficient to meet his normal needs, so that funds with which to repay would be still to seek. To lenders, to potential lenders, that would be very obvious. An unsecured loan to the State would thus be in the same class as unsecured loans to private persons with no credit—very risky lending, which would not be undertaken voluntarily, save possibly at usurious rates.

The State, in the Middle Phase, was as a rule not credit-worthy. This was only in part a consequence of the inelasticity of tax revenue, which made it difficult to repay when the time came for repayment. It was only too easy, when that time came, to rationalize default. These people say that they have lent the money; but why did they not pay it over in tax? They had shown, by lending, that they had the money; so it was easy for the King and his servants to persuade themselves, when the time came, that it was money which ought to have been contributed outright. The bond would be there; but if the Royal debtor was recalcitrant, how was it to be enforced? To use the Sovereign's own courts for the enforcement of a claim against him would be difficult, and might well be impossible. Lending to the State was thus, in general, more risky than lending to private persons.

From this dilemma (as in the analogous case of lending to private persons) there would however, as we have seen, be ways of escape. If unsecured borrowing was difficult, or ruin-ously expensive, what about secured borrowing? Here (and indeed particularly here) it is important to distinguish between the two kinds.[1] Borrowing upon mortgage (in which the 'security' remains in the hands of the debtor) would not in this case be much encouragement to the lender; for if the debtor defaulted, it would still be necessary to have recourse to the courts to enforce the claim, and it is not obvious that this would here be any easier than in the case of the unsecured loan. The position is somewhat different with respect to the other kind, for if the creditor has possession of his 'gage' he is in a stronger position. Thus it may still be possible to have recourse to the pawnshop. It is to the pawnshop (in the widest sense) that we find Middle Phase governments, time and time again, having to turn.

I am not just thinking of pawning the Crown jewels (though

[1] See above, pp. 74–6.

that has happened). Pawning is the actual handing over of an asset, to be returned when the loan is repaid, but remaining in the meantime in the hands of the lender. (He can never be sure, in the case of a loan to the State, that what is handed over will not be taken back by force; but this is a lesser risk than he faces with other forms of lending.) The asset that is pawned may be landed property—royal estates; but it may (and perhaps more often does) take less tangible forms. It may consist in the right to collect certain taxes (tax-farming very largely begins as a form of royal borrowing); it may take the form of a right to appointment to certain offices. There is indeed not much difference between pawning an asset, with little prospect of redemption, and outright sale. Thus borrowing against a tax-farm slides into selling tax-farms; and that slides into selling exemptions from future taxation. All of these methods have been used, but their history is not a happy one; there are numerous instances in which their use has led to disaster.

Long-continued recourse to the tax-exemption method tends to result in a situation where the poor are still paying taxes, while the rich (who purchased exemption in the past) are largely exempt; a condition which has become a regular symbol of rottenness in finance, associated with the fall of the monarchy in France and perhaps in Russia also. Parting with State property, and parting with taxing power, obviously weaken government. We can trace their effects in the ruin of Charlemagne's empire, and in the ruin of the Holy Roman Empire of Germany that succeeded it. It is the same story under the early Stuarts in England.[1] It would not be surprising if it were a part of the explanation of that greatest of historical mysteries, the decline and fall of the original Roman Empire itself.[2]

[1] Vivid details are given in Mrs. Prestwich's *Cranfield* (Oxford 1966), esp. Chs. 1, 8.

[2] The financial history of the Roman Empire is (not surprisingly) one of its darkest aspects. We know what taxes were supposed to be collected, but we do not know what they yielded, nor much about the ways in which 'extraordinary' expenditure was covered. What is known does nevertheless seem to fit without obvious straining into the theoretical pattern.

The government of Augustus was clearly a rich government, very adequately financed, partly from the 'rents' of confiscated estates, partly from a relatively

It may nevertheless be asked: 'Why was it necessary for monarchs to have recourse to such desperate measures, when they had an alternative not so far considered?' We have already seen that all this while the money was the King's money; why should he not, by manipulating the money supply, have got himself out of his difficulties? The answer is, of course, that very often he did attempt to do so; there were plenty of currency inflations (by debasement or otherwise) even in the days of metallic currency. Not all of the secular decline in the value of so many monetary units, in terms of gold and silver, is to be ascribed to the neediness of princes; but some considerable part is clearly to be attributed to that cause. Nevertheless, in spite of the decline which is so clearly visible when we make comparisons across the centuries, money was more stable in those days, much more stable than we have

efficient tax system, which, when spread over so vast an area and so large a population, imposed a burden that was by no means intolerable. It was nevertheless to be expected, in Middle Phase conditions (which here apply), that a system of this kind, even if it started well, would in time run down. In the Roman case the decline was slow. In the first two centuries of the Empire major wars (external or internal) were rather uncommon; financial erosion could therefore proceed at a very moderate pace. It would nevertheless have proceeded, even if slowly; and after a point (which seems to have been reached in the reign of Marcus Aurelius) the pace would quicken. What happens then (in the third century A.D.) is not primarily barbarian invasion, but the collapse of Roman government.

But it is government that perishes in such convulsions, not (or not necessarily) the society over which that government has ruled. The emergency is similar to that which (as we have seen) would swing a pre-mercantile economy in a 'command' direction; and that is what seems to have happened in the Roman case. The 'feudalism' that has been detected in the institutions of the New Empire (of Diocletian and Constantine) is, in the circumstances, a natural reaction. By confiscations, and other exactions, a revenue is reconstituted; but hardly has it been reconstituted when it is subjected to erosion in its turn. And this time (for the New Empire does not have the luck of the old) the erosion is quicker.

It may indeed be said that this is to read the history of Rome as if it was the history of China: to equate the fall of Rome more exactly than is appropriate with the (nearly contemporary) fall of the Han. It does nevertheless seem illuminating to recognize that there is a parallel. It is true that there are differences, and the differences may well be more important than the similarities. The classical bureaucracy of China was able to recreate itself, after each collapse, and to return to the old paths. Europe, when it rose again from darker Dark Ages, replayed the old drama, but played it (as we have already seen) in a decidedly different way.

found it to be in our time. This is not only a matter of the stability of the 'great' currencies which were widely used in international or distant commerce—that proud sequence which begins with the solidus of Constantine, continues with the nomisma of the Byzantines, the dinar and dirhem of the Arabs, the florin of Florence, the ducat of Venice, leading on to the gulden of Holland and the pound sterling—currencies which maintained their value for centuries, sometimes many centuries, on end.[1] Local currencies, which did not have this general circulation, were much more at the mercy of needy governments. Such local currencies did much more often depreciate; but (even so) not so frequently as on recent experience we might expect.[2]

The explanation, I think, is the following. The issue of money (in the days of gold and silver coinage) depended upon a supply of metal to the Mint. One possible source of supply was the King's own revenue. Having (by this time) got the main part of his revenue into money form, he could send it, on receiving it, to be recoined; there was then an opportunity of reissuing it in a baser form (with more alloy) so as to make it go further. This was always possible, and must on occasion have happened; but in an emergency, when the need for additional funds was greatest, it was not at all convenient. To organize a smooth flow of metal through the Mint was not at all simple; the money was liable to be held up, awaiting recoinage, just when it was wanted to be spent.[3] Thus although this source was a potential vehicle of debasement, it was not so important in practice as one might at first have supposed.

The principal source of metal (in normal times, and—for the above reason, even in emergencies) was the trade source. Dealers finding themselves with a stock of worn coins, or uncoined metal, would bring it to the Mint to be changed into

---

[1] On such a time-scale as this the U.S. dollar hardly counts.

[2] The very general depreciation of 'little' currencies, in the city-states of the Italian Renaissance (while the 'great' currencies remained stable) has been analysed by Professor Cipolla, *Money, Prices, and Civilization in the Mediterranean Area* (New York 1956).

[3] I owe this point to the work of Prof. J. D. Gould on the English inflation under Henry VIII (*The Great Debasement*, Oxford 1969).

a more acceptable form. Minting of this type was a govern-
mental trading activity; the Mint was performing a service,
for which it made a charge (seignorage). The supply was
voluntary; the dealers did not need to bring the metal to the
Mint unless it suited them to do so.

It is in these terms that we can appreciate the distinction
between the 'great' and the local currencies. If an attempt
were to be made to exact additional funds by debasing a
'great' currency, there was a danger that the supply of metal
to the Mint would simply dry up. The money that was required was a money that was to be acceptable over a wider
area than was under the control of the State that owned the
Mint; it was to be acceptable to professional dealers who had
a sharp eye for currency manipulation;[1] so if an attempt were
made to cheat by offering baser money, the suppliers of metal
would just go away. Efforts would, of course, be made to prevent them from turning to another Mint which was outside
this State's jurisdiction; the provisions about exportation of
money and bullion that are so familiar. But it is notoriously
difficult to make such provisions effective; they are not very
effective, even at this day.

A local currency, the circulation of which was confined to
the area which the government controlled, was a different
matter. Such a currency could be made acceptable, by making
it *legal tender*. This did not only mean that supplies of metal,
offered for conversion into local money, would not be cut off
by debasement; it was even possible to stimulate suppliers,
by offering to them a share in the profit.[2] The price (in terms
of local money) which was offered to suppliers could be put
up; though the gain (per unit of silver) that accrued to the
government would be diminished, the total gain would be

[1] A classical example of this sensitivity is the story of Adam of Brescia, who
figures in a famous passage of the Inferno. The coins which he passed were
'buon di peso ma non di lega'—full weight but only 21 carats fine, instead of the
regulation 24. He was nevertheless detected—and burned alive (Toynbee's
Dante Dictionary, art. Adamo, Maestro).

[2] It is worth observing that this motive for debasement would operate whenever
the supply of metal became scarce, for any reason. You had to debase, just to
keep the Mint employed.

increased (and might be largely increased) since the volume of metal that came in for recoinage would be magnified. This, it seems clear, was the mechanism by which the supply of local money was so often manipulated, so as to provide (especially in emergencies) a subsidiary source of revenue.

But this, of course (even in the case of a local currency), was by no means the end of the story. If any considerable use was made of such debasement, prices would be likely to rise; and there would then be a question of the effect of the inflation upon the State's normal revenue. If (as in Middle Phase conditions was quite likely to happen) a large part of normal revenue was fixed in money terms, and could not be raised in money terms without evoking the resistance that was commonly evoked by increased taxes, the effect of the inflation would be to reduce the real value of normal revenue. Inflation, as a source of extraordinary revenue to meet an emergency, would then be no better than the other expedients which I have been describing. Like sale of property, or sale of offices, it would leave the government, when the emergency was over, in a weakened position.

Taxes could indeed be raised, without making their real burden any heavier than it had been in the past; but it is intelligible that it would often be easier to proceed in a different way. Have a currency reform; admit debasement; change the debased coins, at a reduced value, into more full-bodied money; and then insist that it is in terms of this reformed money that the taxes are to be paid. A new monarch could do this, putting the blame upon his predecessors; but the imbroglio, from which he had in this painful manner extricated himself, would be one that in future he himself would be anxious to avoid.[1]

[1] This is in fact what was done by Queen Elizabeth I in 1559. (The practice of basing customs revenue upon valuations that remained unchanged over long periods, meant that a large part of the revenue was in money terms very rigid.)

It is interesting to find that this was in fact the substantial reason (beyond the splendid 'hard money' rhetoric) that was advanced 'at the council table of Charles I' to dissuade that monarch, in spite of his desperate financial straits, from having recourse to currency debasement. See the famous speech, attributed to Sir T. Roe, as given in 1641, but more probably delivered by Sir R. Cotton

This explains how it was that local currencies might temporarily depreciate; and it also explains how it was that the depreciation, even of local currencies, was not as great as we might, on our own experience, have been led to expect. Yet there was a long-run tendency to depreciation; for that there is, I think, another reason. If revenue tended to be rigid in money terms, that was a reason against depreciation; but it might well happen that the more important rigidity was on the other side. A currency reform, such as that just described, implies a recognition that the money which is unit of account (in which debts are expressed) is something different from the physical coinage. If revenue could be written up by revaluing the unit of account, debt could be written down by devaluing it. The downward drift in the value of 'unit of account' monies, so readily distinguishable over the centuries, is surely to be interpreted as a matter of successive partial repudiations. In some of the better documented cases, the repudiation motive is very clear.[1]

It is understandable that rigidity ('in money terms') would sometimes be greater on one side, sometimes on the other; when the rigidity was greater on the expenditure side, there would be a tendency for the value of money to slip, but when it was greater on the revenue side, there would be a period of considerable stability.[2]

in 1626. (It was quoted as Roe's by Henry Thornton in the Bullion debate, but printed as Cotton's by McCulloch in *Old and Scarce Tracts on Money*, London 1856, reprinted 1933. One would guess that the explanation of the mystery is that Roe did in fact deliver a speech in 1641 in the same sense; but the 1641 printer was unable to procure Roe's text, and substituted the speech delivered by Cotton on the earlier occasion.)

I should like to acknowledge the help which I received on this matter from the late Prof. T. S. Ashton.

[1] One sees it quite clearly in the financial history of the French monarchy during the eighteenth century. The *louis* (coin) was written up in terms of the *livre* (unit of account) as a means of extricating the government from financial embarrassment.

[2] The interpretation of currency history in terms of public finance, which I have been adopting in these pages, contrasts with the interpretation in terms of class interests (debtors *versus* creditors) that is common among economic historians. I do not mean to deny that there have been cases in which class interests will have played a part (pressure from agricultural debtors is a common phenomenon, for instance in Greek and Roman history); but I think that before invoking that

I have taken all this trouble to enlarge upon the financial weakness of the typical Middle Phase government, and its causes, partly because it seems to me to explain a wide range of historical phenomena which are otherwise hard to understand; and partly because it throws a striking light upon what has happened afterwards. The financial position of modern governments, *vis à vis* the rest of the economy over which they are set, is immensely stronger; but the strengthening has come about in various ways which need to be distinguished, though they interact. Some go back a fairly long way, being consequences of the development of credit, the beginnings of which I associated (in Chapter V) with the city states of the Renaissance; some are very much more recent.

I begin with a minor improvement in the technique of government borrowing, which had a considerable effect upon the credit-worthiness of governments—or rather, as we shall see, of some governments.

As long as government only borrowed in the simplest way, promising to repay the principal in a year or two—and then, only too obviously, wanting to reborrow for another short period what it was unable to repay—the improbability of its being able to raise from its tax revenue the considerable addition, which would be needed to liquidate the loan in the end, was a serious deterrent to lenders. If, on the other hand, the repayment could be spread over a longer period, a moderate amortization being added to annual interest, the burden became more manageable, and the promise of repayment became more credible. But the credibility of the undertaking would still depend upon the prospect of faith being kept over a long period of time, extending into decades; and it can be appreciated that there would be governments which had need to borrow, but were unable to offer a high probability of such continuity. Royal governments, which depended upon

influence, a means by which it could have been brought to bear should be demonstrated. The *direct* pressures which must have been exerted upon those who had to take the relevant decisions were surely those which came from the condition of the State treasury; it is hard to see that it is usually necessary to go any further in order to get a sufficient explanation of what happened.

the personality of the ruler, were always liable to a sharp change of course upon succession; even when son succeeded father, he might be bitterly opposed to his father's policies, and might have little respect for the debts which, in pursuit of those policies, his father had incurred.[1] Republican governments were actually better placed, since they were less dependent upon the mortal individual. We do in fact find that it was Republican governments which first made considerable use of borrowing upon 'annuity'.[2] The sharp rise in the credit of the British government (marked by the fall in the rate of interest at which it could borrow, from 10 per cent under William III to 3 per cent under Walpole and Pelham) must surely be attributed, among other influences, to the fact that the 'Constitution' of 1689, once it was firmly established, gave to the British monarchy the continuity, and therefore the long-term credit, of a Republic.

A more generally potent influence, however, was the rise of banking. There are three distinct stages in the evolution of banking, of which the first, in which the bank is no more than a financial intermediary, has already been mentioned.[3] People lend to the banker, altogether he pays a lower rate of interest than that which he charges (his 'in-rate' must be lower than his 'out-rate' if he is to make a profit) because they do not have the knowledge, which he has acquired in building up his business, by which they can find for themselves such safe and

---

[1] It could be maintained, in France, as late as 1715, that a king had no obligation to honour the debts of his predecessor (Saint-Simon, *Memoirs*, Pleiade edition, vol. 4, p. 784).

[2] As so often in such matters, the practice goes back to Florence and Venice in the fourteenth century. It is curious, but understandable, that the receipt of an annual income from an irredeemable security was not even then regarded as at all reprehensible, Sapori (op. cit., p. 111) has actually found a Florentine statute of 1415 which laid upon trustees for minors the *duty* of investing trust funds in such annuities 'to yield not less than 5 per cent'. The city states of sixteenth-century Germany used the same method (Ehrenburg, *Capital and Finance in the Age of the Renaissance*, English translation, London 1928, pp. 43–4); so did seventeenth-century Holland. Even in a monarchy, when the king was unable to borrow on such terms, local authorities might do so. There were even attempts by the State to make use of this local credit, as when the French King borrowed 'on the Hôtel de Ville'.

[3] Above, p. 78.

profitable investments as he is finding. Now it might be thought that mere intermediation of this kind would have no effect upon government borrowing—for the need of the government to borrow would be obvious, and would need no expert to find it out. But that is not so; even at this stage the appearance of the intermediary makes quite a difference.

I have explained that the difficulty of enforcing claims against the State was liable to make the State's credit less good than that of (reliable) merchants, against whom claims could readily be enforced. The bank (or other intermediary) is from this point of view quite fully within the regular legal system; loans to the bank are regular commercial loans that fall within the ordinary law. The bank, in lending to the government, does not itself have this protection; but the fact that it can go bankrupt, and would be liable to go bankrupt if the State just defaulted on it, proves in fact to be a protection—of a sort. The failure of a bank, on which it has become accustomed to rely, is a danger that it may be fair to reckon that government will be unwilling to face. It was in this way that the formation of the Bank of England, and of the other great corporations (even the South Sea Company) which played an analogous part in eighteenth-century England, operated as a further means of improving the government's credit.

This, however (inevitably), was no more than a first step.

The second stage of banking evolution comes when the banker realizes that it is safe for him, or usually safe for him, to accept money on deposit, subject to withdrawal on demand or at short notice. Though he is exposed to the danger of a 'run', means that are more or less effective can be taken to guard against it. It is often represented that this reliance upon the insurance principle is the essence of banking. But banks do not have to accept deposits; it is the middleman function which is really primary.

The importance of this second stage is largely that it leads (and often very rapidly leads) to the third, which nevertheless is logically distinguishable from it. This is the point at which deposits in banks, withdrawable deposits, are made transferable: either by cheque, which is an instruction to a bank to transfer an existing deposit, or by note—which is in effect a cheque payable to bearer, having the guarantee of the bank behind it, without reference to the depositor against whose deposit it was originally issued. This is vital; for it is at this point that the bank becomes able to create what is in effect money. When it makes a loan, it does not have to hand out the old 'hard' money; all it does is to exchange claims. Against the obligation of the borrower, to repay by some fixed date, it provides an obligation of its own, which is transferable upon demand, and for that reason has a money quality. The money which it lends is money that it itself creates.

Now the consequence of this, not perceived at first, but in our time become abundantly evident, is that the control of the State over the money supply, which for long ages was so imperfect, has become complete. It is not just a matter of the introduction of paper money, so much cheaper to produce than the old metallic money; for paper money, issued by the State, in the unsuitable environment we have hitherto been considering, would not have worked.[1] It is the channel of money creation that is provided by the banking system which makes the difference. There is no longer a danger of the State's defaulting, on debt expressed in its own currency, since it is always possible for it to borrow from the banking system; the banks are not able to refuse to lend, since they can always create money to finance their loans. The power that thus passes into the hands of the State is very great, but by itself it is not unlimited. I need not enlarge upon that; for this is the point in our story when we come to the Age of Keynes, that new dispensation under which since 1936 we know that we have been living. The lesson that Keynes taught was of the existence of the power that I have just described. It already existed, and Keynes had only to urge that it should be taken

[1] Governments did indeed try to issue paper to pay their armies, but the soldiers did not take it well. It was simply regarded as an IOU that might possibly be honoured at some (very uncertain) future date.
Things may have been different in China (see above, p. 68); but this, I think, was the European experience.

up. But sometimes he gives the impression that he thought it had always existed;[1] and that, I feel sure, is not right. It did already exist when he was writing, but it had not existed for so very long. It is not in the nature of things; it is a consequence of the development of modern banking. It is another of the ways in which contemporary economies have passed from what I have been calling the Middle Phase into a characteristically Modern Phase.

Taken by itself, the Monetary Power is one that can only too easily be misused, or over-used. The inflation which results from its over-use can be carried to extreme lengths under the new dispensation, such as in the old days of predominantly metallic currency was hardly possible. If it is temperately used, it can be a means of control; over-used, it is a threat to control. If the State had no economic power except this monetary power, it would not be able to dominate the Mercantile Economy, as it has come to dominate it.

For it is not only in this monetary way that the power of the State has been increased, in the later stages of financial development; and perhaps it is not even the most important way. The Mercantile Economy can escape from purely monetary inflation, by adjusting itself to it;[2] it can do its calculations on the assumption of continued inflation, so that after all not much is changed *in real terms*. Besides, it is still no more than the local (or national) money that the State is manipulating; there is an international money—the lineal successor of the florin and the ducat of former ages—which remains out of reach. From the beginning of the present century, governments have refused to coin that money, and have thus restricted its circulation; they have endeavoured to canalize its use into transactions between themselves, or between the Central Banks that represent them. Yet so long as there are transactions which cross the boundaries of the jurisdictions of particular states, the national money is not enough; there is always a need for international money, in

---

[1] As in his rhetorical passages about pyramids—and mediaeval cathedrals!

[2] The high rates of interest, to which we are becoming accustomed in the nineteen-sixties, are the most obvious adjustment.

some form or other. The Balance of Payments is the point of clash between the national money, which the State now controls, and the international money which—by itself—it cannot.

It may thus be more important that there are other ways by which the State has been economically strengthened. We have already seen that the taxing power of the State, which for long ages was so rudimentary, has in these last two centuries been immensely fortified. The income taxes, the profits taxes, the sales taxes, even the capital taxes such as death duties, which have today become so important as sources of government revenue, are only possible because of the financial development, some aspects of which I have been describing. It is because incomes arise out of legal contracts, enforceable at law, that they can be established at law, and can therefore be taxed. It is because profits—nowadays the great bulk of profits—are the profits of companies, which are complicated legal entities, operating under closely prescribed legal provisions, that profits are taxable, indeed so readily taxable. It is because so large a part of property is now in the form of transferable securities, with easily established market prices, that capital taxes, of any degree of efficiency, are feasible at all. In all of these ways the taxing power of the State has been fortified by mercantile development—as is evident, in our own day, by the difficulty experienced by many 'underdeveloped' countries in generating a tax revenue that is adequate for their purposes. Their difficulty is not just one of poverty; it is also due to the fact that so much of the wealth that some of their people do possess is out of their government's reach.

These things interact; for it is also important that these modern taxes, being so much more closely geared to current transactions than those which were the only possible taxes in the Middle Phase, have a quite different response to inflation. A progressive income tax, in particular, actually raises more *real* revenue on an unchanged tax formula, when there is a rise in prices and money incomes; unlike the old taxes, based upon assessments that were sticky in money terms, which (as we have seen) raised less. The backlash on normal revenue, which in the old conditions made inflation a danger to government, is therefore removed. This is surely a major reason why modern governments (or some modern governments) take inflation so calmly. If they have a strong tax administration, they can afford to do so. But this cannot be the only cause of modern inflationism, as is made evident by the South American example. The tax administrations of such countries as Argentina and Brazil are clearly unable to cope with the inflation that they practise.

There does indeed remain, in addition to the monetary and fiscal matters on which I have discoursed at length, the pure point of administrative efficiency. It is impossible to have a strong administration—a large and inquisitive administration—unless it can be paid for; the State must be able to pay, since otherwise it cannot have the officials through whom to rule. But the 'amount' of control that can be 'purchased' for a given expenditure may be large or may be small; there can be no doubt that in the Modern Phase it has been very sharply increased. The change that has ensued is so important, and so potent, that we cannot get on without naming it; I shall call it (together with the other changes which as we have seen are associated with it) the *Administrative Revolution*. It is partly a matter of organization—direct improvements in the application of the division of labour; but it is partly (as in the case of the *Industrial Revolution*) a matter of the application of capital equipment. Modern governments, one would guess, over-use the aeroplane; but where would they be without the telephone—and the typewriter? The contribution of the computer to this mechanization of government is only beginning to be seen. It is already the case that it would be easier (technically) to govern New Zealand from London than it was to govern Scotland from London in the eighteenth century.

All this can be said, it will be noticed, without uttering a word about Socialism—or about *laissez-faire*. Nor was it necessary to make distinctions about political structure— about the ways in which those who rule are selected, or select themselves. Continuity, as we have seen, is important; but if

79989

continuity is achieved, it does not matter how it is achieved. I am not, of course, saying that these political matters are unimportant. They affect the way in which power is used, but they do not have much to do with the generation of the power itself. It is perfectly possible that a government may have power which (for ideological or other reasons) it prefers not to use. It remains true that it cannot use a power which, in the state of society in which it is operating, it does not possess.

So far then, only so far, the story which I have been elaborating falls into shape. The Mercantile Economy, in its First Phase, was an escape from political authority—except in so far as it made its own political authority. Then, in the Middle Phase, when it came formally back under the traditional political authority, that authority was not strong enough to control it. It might destroy, but it could not control. In the Modern Phase, into which we have now passed, that is changed. Largely because of the internal evolution of the Mercantile Economy, control over it has become immensely easier. This is so, whatever is the political structure, and whatever are the ends of the controllers. Their powers will serve them alike for War or Peace, for the solving of social problems or for smothering them.

VII

THE MERCANTILIZATION OF AGRICULTURE

I HAD better begin this chapter by reminding the reader why it is only now, at this rather late stage in my enquiry, that I come to the Factors of Production, Land and Labour, and to the Forms of Production, Agriculture and Industry. No one questions that Land and Labour are the foundations upon which any economy, however organized, must be based; and that some kind of food production, and some kind of non-food production, are characteristics of almost any economy. These things are as true of the market economy as of any other. It remains the case that the Market, as a form of organization, is the creation of traders and subsequently financiers, not (or not at all to the same extent) of farmers or of artisans. The commodity markets and the financial markets are the places where the market system is at home; when it proceeds to the formation of factor markets, land and labour markets, it is penetrating, or 'colonizing', relatively refractory territory. This was territory where its principles did not fit, or could only with difficulty be made to fit. Thus there was a struggle, which begins very early, and continues (though in forms which are undergoing significant changes) into our own day.

I begin with agriculture. There was a pre-existing agricultural system: the *lord and peasant system*, I think we must call it[1]—the principal variant of the command-customary

[1] We need something more general, and more specifically agricultural, than 'Feudalism'. Marc Bloch's 'Seignorial system' (see his classic chapter in the *Cambridge Economic History of Europe*, vol. 1, either edition) was clearly introduced with the same purpose as I have in mind, and it is tempting. It might do, in

system, considered in its agricultural aspect. This was very ancient, and was very strong. It was strong because it met a real need. Lord and peasant were necessary to each other, and the land, the same land, was necessary to both. The peasant was necessary to the lord, since it was from a share in the peasant's produce that he derived his support; and there was a corresponding way in which the lord was necessary to the peasant. Whatever the burden that was laid upon him, he got something in return; and what he got in return was vital. What he got was Protection.

Merchants, as we have seen, met their needs for protection by congregating in towns; but though the peasant might get some personal protection by forming villages, he could not in that way protect his crops. The growing of crops takes time. There is an interval, at least of months, between the input of labour, or some of the input of labour, and the appearance of the disposable or consumable product that results from it. During that interval, and especially towards the end of that interval, the farmer who is on his own is in an exposed position. He cannot, by himself, protect the fruits of his labour (which, if they are to be sufficient for his support, must be spread over an appreciable area); he cannot protect them adequately against raiders, or against thieves. Someone, somehow, must be found to give him that protection.

Why, it may however be asked, should the need not be met by co-operation among the peasants themselves? Sometimes this may be the answer; but most generally it is not an efficient answer. For here, as in other matters, there is an advantage in division of labour; some nucleus, at least, of a standing army (even of 'retainers'[1]) makes defence more effective.

It can indeed be granted that there are circumstances in which the need for protection is not acute. Farms that are established in inaccessible places, as in mountainous country,

French; but in England it is too suggestive of the particular form of the system that was prevalent in the Middle Ages in Western Europe. We need something which does not simply suggest that, but is readily extensible, when required, to the boyars of Russia or the daimyo of Japan.

[1] or samurai.

may not be in much danger of attack, or even of pilfering. The road to independent farming is in such cases fairly clear. The 'free peasant' of the mountains is a well-known phenomenon.

It is of more general importance that there is one kind of farming where there is bound to be less need of specialized protection. 'And there were shepherds, abiding in the fields, keeping watch over their flocks by night.' Whether they are in the 'fields' or in shelters, it is the principal business of the pastoralist, in the technical conditions that have obtained until very lately, to be the guardian of his flocks and herds. He is himself a specialist protector, fairly efficient by himself against wild beasts or against thieves. In the case of greater dangers his mobility makes it easier for him to combine with his fellows.

There are these exceptions; but I do not think they make it wrong to regard the open-country arable cultivation, and the lord-and-peasant system which for so long belonged to it, as the characteristic form of pre-mercantile agriculture. It is upon that form that the mercantilization, which we shall be studying, has worked the most thoroughgoing transformation.

There is another organizational need, as well as the need for defence, which has to be met in some way or other. This is the need for the settlement of disputes between neighbours. In the mountains, where one plot is well separated from another, this is at a minimum; but when plots are contiguous, there is the trouble that natural processes do not stop at artificial boundaries. The boundary itself must first be established; some form of jurisdiction is needed to establish it.[1] Even when it is established nature will not respect it. What is sown on one plot comes up on another; the weeds that arise from the neglect of one are a curse to its neighbours. It is the protecting power that can enforce its decisions; so it comes to pass, in the lord-and-peasant system, that the Protector is also a judge.[2]

---

[1] 'Limes agro positus *litem* ut discerneret arvis', as Virgil puts it.

[2] Since the (old-style) *pastoral* community can hold its lands in common, these questions do not arise, to any important extent, within the group; but they do arise when there is contact with other groups, as matters of external relations. The mating of the native 'scrub cattle' with the superior breeds brought in by the settlers is said to have been a prime cause of the early 'Kaffir wars' in South Africa.

8—T.E.H.

Now it will, of course, be said that Justice and Defence are functions of the State; we take it for granted nowadays that the State will perform them. But the appearance of a government that is strong enough to perform them adequately is not a thing which happens automatically. To look for the adequate performance of these functions from the governments of our Middle Phase, weak both financially and administratively, would usually have been impossible. No more is needed to explain the persistence of a lord-and-peasant system over many centuries, in many places almost up to modern times.

It did not only persist; it recreated itself, under suitable conditions, when there had been a move away from it. There had been room under the Roman Peace, in some places at least, for a (more or less) free peasantry; but as the Empire declined the formerly free peasants 'commended' themselves to a lord. It was necessary for them to find a Protector; when the Empire failed, some local chief had to do.

The impact of the market on the lord-and-peasant system takes place in two stages, which must be distinguished. In the first stage there is commercial penetration only; in the second, which is the more important, there is financial penetration as well.

On the stage of commercial penetration I have little to add to what has been said in previous chapters. It may well begin by the peasant himself doing a little trading with pedlars, and on country markets; but we shall expect (in accordance with what has been said formerly) that it will be the trading of the lord himself, through his servants, which will be more important as an agent of change. As we have seen, he is enabled by trading to turn his revenue into a form which is more acceptable to him than that in which it appears when it is simply a share in what is produced, on their own fields, by his own peasants. And it will be still easier for him to do this when he can get his revenue into a money form. But in order that the peasants' dues should be paid in money, they have got to get money. So it is to the lord's interest, once that point is reached, to encourage his peasants to sell their produce to traders for money, some of which they will no doubt spend themselves, while the rest is paid over to the lord.

At the commercial stage, that is all that need happen; but it is worth observing, before passing on, that the motive for this first movement towards the market is the same as that which leads, in not very different circumstances, in the opposite direction. There is another way in which the lord may get his revenue in a more acceptable form than that which comes to him as a share in what is produced on the peasants' holdings; this is to reserve a part of the land (demesne land, in the mediaeval European application) for cultivation in a manner which is more closely under his own control. What is to be produced on this land he can more exactly determine; and he has a better chance of getting the produce when he wants it, not just at the times when it is customary or conventional for the peasants to bring it in. Land, however, needs labour to work it; there will be no labour to work the lord's land unless the peasants pay a part of their dues in direct services. (He may indeed cultivate his land by labour which is in his direct employment; but such labour has to be fed, and it may well be easiest to let them feed themselves by giving them their own plots; so this method, in effect, is liable to come out to much the same thing.)

A lord-and-peasant system that moves in this direction would generally be regarded as moving towards a more complete condition of serfdom; while the alternative route, of encouraging the peasant to produce for the market, looks relatively liberating. The two may nevertheless intertwine. It is perfectly possible (and indeed very likely) that marketable produce may be more easily and efficiently produced upon the lord's land, where the peasants work under supervision, than upon the land of the peasants. The opening of the market will then increase the advantage (to the lord) of more direct farming; he will move, so far as he can, in the direction of exacting his revenue in the form of labour services, getting his money income by the sale of his 'own' produce to the market, not in the form of money dues paid to him by 'his' peasants.

It must nevertheless be insisted that nothing has yet

happened, on either of these routes, to upset the foundation of the lord-and-peasant system; lord and peasant remain necessary to one another, and the land is necessary to both. But it is becoming appropriate to think of their relation in terms of exchange; though if we allow ourselves to think of it in that way, the only type of exchange which fits is that of simple exchange without competition, or bilateral monopoly. Under bilateral monopoly, the textbooks tell us, the terms of exchange are 'indeterminate'; which means that they are settled, so we are given to understand, by the will of the stronger. One must suppose that in this application the lord is the stronger; there is no question that the peasant is at a bargaining disadvantage. But what this means, so far, should not be exaggerated. The lord, by exercising pressure, can move the 'bargaining' in his favour; he can do so at any time, but if he is to continue to make extra extortions, the pressure must be kept up. If it is relaxed, the peasants will slip back into giving no more than they think to be customary. That is their defence: their passive resistance.

It is probable that the lord is in a stronger position, more able to increase his revenue when he desires, by using pressure, when he has taken either of the steps we have been considering, than he was when he simply relied upon a share in the produce of the peasant's holding. For a share in produce is not easy to assess, easiest when there is concentration upon a single crop, much harder as soon as there is diversification. So long as he keeps to his customary proportion, he can rely upon the peasants policing one another; for if one of them holds back, the others will feel that he is cheating them. But if he tries to raise his claim, all will consider themselves entitled to cheat. A money payment is more easily enforceable, and so is the exaction of so many days' direct labour.[1]

These are the first steps; yet when they have been taken, the lord-and-peasant system is still, in its essentials, intact. Land and peasant, and lord, are still tied together. Even when the peasant has established some connection with the market, he

---

[1] It may indeed be granted that thirty days' labour, given under protest, may yield no more than twenty that are (relatively) willingly given.

remains tied to the soil (*adscriptus glebae*, as the old law books put it); and it is of equal importance that the soil is tied to him. There is, as yet, no land *ownership*. The lord has rights in the land, and the peasant has rights in the land; but that is all. It is of much concern to them what these rights are; but it does not need to be made clear to any outsider. The rights are established by custom; it is to custom that an appeal will be made whenever they are challenged.

It will, of course, happen now and then that an estate changes hands by inheritance on the death of a particular lord, or as an endowment to a royal servant or religious foundation. The rights of lordship, whatever they are, will then pass to the new possessor; it will be up to him to find out, by experience, just what the rights are with which he has been endowed. There is as yet no market in land; it is only occasionally, and with difficulty, that land can be sold.

One would guess that before it is sold, or at all often sold, it will be pledged. When financial development has gone far enough for it to be possible to raise loans, the lords of estates will find it easier to borrow if they can use their lands as security for borrowing. But rights in land, that are purely customary, are a poor security to the lender; for it will be a mystery to him just what he can expect to get in the case of default. The land will be a better security if the rights of lordship are set down in black and white, in terms that men of business, and lawyers, can understand. Thus there is at this point an incentive for the lord to get his rights *defined*—not only at the moment when he seeks to pledge his land (or to sell it), but as soon as he begins to contemplate the possibility that he may want to do so at some time or other.

It is not possible to define the rights of the lord without defining the rights of the peasant also. But it is very intelligible that an arrangement that is made by the lord, with the aid of lawyers, looking (for that is the point of making the arrangement) not at the needs of the peasant but at those of a potential lender or potential buyer, should be an arrangement in which the interests of the peasant are inclined to be overlooked. There must be a tendency that way—to convert the lord's rights into something which is more or less in line with the concept of property as understood by the merchant. But if the land is made the lord's property, in that sense, how are the rights of the peasant to find a place?

Even previously, as we have seen, the peasant was at a bargaining disadvantage; but now, when matters that concern him intimately are being settled 'over his head', his disadvantage is intensified. He is almost bound to lose some of his former rights; but it is of immense importance that he may lose them, in different conditions, in significantly different ways.

Whoever is to be the owner of the land, someone must cultivate it; land which cannot be cultivated would be valueless, even in the strictest market sense.[1] A prospect of securing the labour that is needed for cultivation, in some way or other, is an element in the value that is set upon the land.

Thus it makes a great deal of difference to the process we are considering whether it takes place in conditions when labour to till the land is relatively plentiful, or in conditions when labour is scarce.[2] When the cultivation of land has been fully mercantilized, labour shortage or abundance will simply reflect itself in the level of rents (and of wages); but the point when that happens is one which we have not yet reached. The question before us is the effect of relative scarcity of labour upon the mercantilization process.

Even when labour (in general) is abundant, there is still a question that has to be faced by the potential purchaser of land (or lender upon landed security); how is he to draw an income from the land which he acquires, or may acquire? It will clearly be simpler for him when the dues of the peasants, upon the estates to be acquired, have been converted into

---

[1] The use of land for pleasure purposes (as for hunting) is a complication which in an outline analysis may fairly be left aside.

[2] Adjustment of agricultural techniques, to meet changes in the relative scarcities of land and labour, is a matter to which we shall come; I assume that at the present stage it still lies ahead. Relatively to given technique, a condition of labour shortage is fairly easily distinguishable. In all probability it is here the exceptional case; but it does arise.

money rents. But how (coming in as an outsider) is he to enforce the payment of those rents? He will look for a sanction; and the only sanction that is available to him, and that he can understand, is dispossession. The rent payment, to him, is in the nature of a contract; if the peasant does not carry out his share of the contract, as interpreted in terms of the new legally enforceable rights, he must go.

That is the mercantile viewpoint; but it arises out of an atmosphere that is so different from that which preceded it, in this matter of land tenure, that it can hardly make headway without a struggle. I have insisted that the lord-and-peasant system had its origin in the need of the peasant for security; but now, in the evolution of the system, his security comes under threat. But the need for security in agriculture is not only social; it is also technological. If the peasant is liable to be dispossessed at any moment, or feels himself liable to be dispossessed at any moment, he cannot embark upon processes of production that take time; so he cannot produce. This is a constraint which even our newcomer must come to understand. Even the fullest mercantilization of agriculture must accordingly incorporate some arrangement for a minimum of security.

The need of the landlord (as we may now call him) for a sanction, and the need of the peasant for security, can both be met; but only by a compromise. The characteristic compromise is the leasing of land for a period of years: tenant farming. Perpetual tenancy, with no more than the right of eviction on non-payment of rent, would be an attractive alternative from the point of view of the tenant; but it is less attractive to the landlord,[1] and in the conditions of labour abundance, which we are still supposing, it is unlikely that the peasant will have the bargaining power to secure it. The landlord cannot draw his rent without giving some security; but he does not have to give more than is strictly necessary.

---

[1] What is to happen when the peasant dies? Though he himself may be a 'good' tenant, he may pass on his holding, if he has the power of bequest, to someone who is less 'good'. Life tenancy, in favourable circumstances, is a just possible arrangement; but hardly more than that, short of outright ownership.

This, then, is one of the things which may happen; but the development of tenant farming is no more than one of the possible alternatives. It may well be more attractive, still in conditions of labour abundance, to develop the arrangement (which, as we have seen, had already made a start under the old system) of farming under the supervision of an overseer or bailiff: direct farming on what, even under the old system, was the lord's own land. This is an important alternative, even here; but it is still more important under the other condition, of labour scarcity, to which I now come.

Labour scarcity, here, is scarcity relatively to land. Thus labour which had been abundant may become scarce, either because of an increase in the supply of land (new land opened up) or because of a fall in the supply of labour. There are plenty of examples of the first,[1] while of the second there is a major example that is highly relevant to our discussion—the fall in population which seems to have occurred in many parts of Europe (as a result of the Black Death and other associated catastrophes) in the fourteenth century A.D. Either of these changes would lead, in a fully mercantilized agriculture, to a fall in rents and a rise in wages—or at least to a rise in wages relatively to rents. But in the conditions we are here considering, when agriculture is no more than semi-mercantilized, or on the eve of mercantilization, the effect may well be different.

It is possible, at the one extreme, that landlords, finding their rent-income reduced (by the departure of some of their peasants to work the new lands, or—as in the fourteenth-century case—by actual death of the peasants) will, because of their financial difficulties, be more eager to sell. But how are they to find a buyer? If lands merely change hands at lower prices than formerly, but to much the same sorts of people, the process we have been discussing will just continue; but it is conceivable that in the circumstances the best

[1] But, most often, it is only labour to till the new land which then becomes scarce; for enough labour to be drawn off to cause a labour shortage on the old land is a much rarer phenomenon.

buyers will be the peasants themselves. There is no reason why there should be a fall in the value of what can be produced on a given plot by land *and* labour; so that although the peasant himself does not have the money to buy out his landlord, he is in a position (or will be in a position when he has acquired his land) to give security, or some sort of security, for a loan. If this is the route that is followed, the lord-and-peasant system will have given way to a free peasantry—a peasantry that is burdened by debt (of which more later) but which is no longer tied to a lord in the way it had been in the former time.

It is possible, again, that a solution may be found by a development of direct farming. Not that a movement in this direction is likely as a reaction to a shortage of labour, but that the direct farming system may be better able to stand up to a shortage of labour than a lord-and-peasant system of the old sort. It is unlikely, now, that sufficient labour for cultivation of the estate will be obtainable from the old direct services; labour will have to be wage-labour, and with the labour market beginning to be competitive, the wage that will have to be paid will be relatively high. Yet high-paid labour, if well managed, can be more than formerly efficient labour. The high wages are a spur to efficiency, and improvements that make for efficiency are more easily introduced on an estate that is managed directly than on the custom-ridden plots of the former peasants.

There are these two directions of what, from different standpoints, may be regarded as 'progress'. They are essentially different but they can nevertheless be combined, and combined with the system of tenant farming, in various ways. What is essential for improvement in efficiency is that the unit of management should be adequate, and that the labour employed should be reasonably well paid. This could occur on the lord's estate in the manner just described, but it could also occur in other ways. It might occur through aggregation of peasant holdings (the more efficient buying out the less efficient); or through a landlord's policy of aggregating tenant farms, more efficient farms being able to pay higher rents. The freer the market in land (to buy and to rent) the more easily would any of these processes operate.

There is, however, no reason why a shortage of labour should necessarily lead in these (at least in the long run constructive) directions. Instead of allowing wages to rise—and then adjusting themselves to the higher wages by one or other of the methods which we have been discussing—would not the landlords be better advised from their own point of view to stop the rise in wages? The simple imposition of maximum wages, though it was tried in the historical case,[1] was bound to be ineffective; the source of the rise in wages was competition for labour; it is competition for labour that must be stopped. The labourer, or peasant-labourer, must be tied to the soil, or re-tied to the soil; in a more exact sense than before, he must be made a serf.

It was already the case in most parts of Western Europe, even in the fourteenth century, that the mercantilization of agriculture had gone too far for the road to serfdom to be open. Or perhaps it was just that even after the fall in population, the land was closely enough settled for movement to a place where the labourer could get 'lost' to be relatively easy. Attempts were indeed made to impose bans on movement, but they did not have much success.[2] In Eastern Europe, however, it was quite another story.

This is not simply the story of Russian serfdom, which is no more than a part of a process that was much more general. There was a general movement in the same direction, not only in Russia but in Central Europe and in Poland—and in Eastern Germany. It is indeed the East German case which is the best documented, so that the sequence of events is most clearly discernible.[3] Eastern Germany, Germany east of the Elbe, had in the twelfth and thirteenth centuries been a

[1] 'Incomes policy' was no more effective in the days of the Statutes of Labourers (passed by the English Parliament—of course a landlords' Parliament—between 1350 and 1380) than it is to-day.

[2] There were such bans in some of the Statutes of Labourers (Clapham, *Concise Economic History of Britain*, Cambridge 1949, p. 111).

[3] I draw upon the excellent account in F. L. Carsten, *The Origin of Prussia* (Oxford 1954).

colonial area into which labour was being drawn from the Rhineland and even from the Low Countries. The German nobility, or their agents, acted as entrepreneurs or land developers, offering favourable terms to attract peasants who, in the first place, became tenant farmers paying rents that were no more than a reasonable return on the costs of development[1] and earning the money to pay those rents by exporting a part of their produce. While the expansion continued these favourable conditions persisted; but in the contraction which followed it, they broke down. With the fall in the population of Europe (for it was no less) the new lands became extra-marginal; in a free market—if that is conceivable upon the large scale that would have been necessary—there would have been a reflux of population from the colonial areas to fill the gaps that had been left 'nearer home'. The landlords, in any case, were in trouble; if there had been a reflux, or any tendency to a reflux, their plight would have been even worse. The peasant must therefore be caught and tied down. In the East of Europe but not, on the whole, in the West, the landlords were strong enough to do it, or were in a position to do it.[2]

The decline in population, which was the occasion for this parting of the ways, was itself a transitory phenomenon; in a couple of generations, or a little longer, it had probably been made up. But the habits and the social institutions which had grown up as a reaction to it were not easily eradicated. Prussia and Poland and Russia remained for centuries in the grip of a nobility of landlords, extracting what revenue they could from poor peasants whom they kept dependent on them; defending as their lifeline an oppressive system which they were unwilling to reform for fear that the house of cards they had built would fall on their heads. Even in the West something of the same sort sometimes happened; but the way had usually

[1] It was often laid down that no rent was to be payable until a period of grace had elapsed—a concession similar to that which some modern governments give to 'pioneer industries'.
[2] It was upon the great plains of Eastern Europe that the peasants were particularly powerless. There are terrible stories of the hunts that were organized by Russian landlords for fugitive peasants.

been kept open for something more elastic. The freer systems did indeed have their own problems, but they were not so closed to the discovery of new ways of solving them.[1]

I turn to consider a question, which is forcibly thrown up by what has just been said about Eastern Europe, but which was probably worrying (and perhaps annoying) the reader even before we reached that point. I began by giving the landlord a function—the function of Protector—but it is surely the case that the processes we have been examining could not go far without that function becoming, at least to a considerable extent, out of date. The market penetration, which we have been examining, was itself a legal penetration; law and order go together; if the State is strong enough to enforce the contracts which have wrought the transformations so far noted, why is it not strong enough to provide the local security on which the 'right' of the landlord has hitherto depended? It can indeed be answered that the two are different: that the respect of men of property for judicial decisions is sufficient for the one, but it in no way implies the existence of an administration which is capable of policing the other. There is a phase (perhaps a lengthy phase) in which the first is operative, or largely operative, while the second remains out of reach. A point must nevertheless arrive[2] when the State becomes capable, or usually capable, of enforcing local order, at least as well as it could be enforced by a local magnate. When that point is reached, what is left of the landlord's 'right'?

It is possible that the landlords will then be superseded, and the State take over. But the fact that supersession is possible does not necessarily mean that it will occur. It cannot occur without something in the nature of a revolution; a

[1] It is no more than a coincidence that the frontier which so long separated these agricultural systems has so striking a resemblance to the Curtain which is dividing Europe at the present day. It can be no more than a coincidence; yet the long experience that has moulded men's minds in one way on one side, and in another on the other, has an effect that is recognizable today, even when the division is expressed in very different terms.

[2] In accordance with what was said about the economic development of the State in Chapter VI.

State may be strong, but it may not care for revolutions. Thus, even though the landlords have lost their function, they may remain. They may continue to draw the revenues which support them as an ornamental aristocracy, though it would now be possible to do without them. This is a condition which may last, and on occasion has lasted, for generations; but if the State has the power to take over, it is likely in the end to have the will.

Even across revolutions, as I have insisted, there is continuity; the continuity which persists in this case is very strong. Whatever the form of the new arrangement, the substance remains—that the State has taken the place of the landlord; so the alternatives before it, and those which were formerly before the landlord, are much the same. It may confine itself to making a 'Land Reform' such as was made at the French Revolution and (since 1945) in so many other countries, establishing the peasant in the more or less complete 'ownership' of his land and reserving for itself no more than the minimum duties of a Protector. Even so, it must exact a payment for its services; the taxes that are paid to the State take the place of the rent that was paid to the landlord in the former time. It may proceed, at the other extreme, to develop a system of state farming—which is just a development, upon a larger scale, of the direct farming which (as we have seen) was commonly practised by the old-style private landlord upon his 'demesne'.

Thus there is a line that persists, even across Revolutions, between what may be described as Independent and Dependent Farming. It is not a matter of ownership; how then is it to be defined?

There is a type of decision which has to be made, in some way or other, in every kind of agriculture, and which can only be made by someone who is in close touch with what is going on. It is the decision 'when'. When to plough, when to plant, when to harvest, when to take measures against pests—with corresponding decisions in animal husbandry. The processes of nature (including the weather) are not in general dependable enough for these decisions to be taken entirely by rule;

though custom gives guidance, someone in the end has to take the responsibility. It will not be misleading if we call that person the farmer; and the productive processes which he in this sense controls, rather than the land on which they are situated, his farm. A farm, so defined, may be large or small according to the type of production and to geographical conditions; the farmer may or may not have other persons who work under his direction. The question of his independence or dependence is not concerned with these matters; it is a question of his freedom to take decisions outside the narrow range of the decisions *when* which cannot be taken, or cannot altogether be taken, out of his responsibility. The most important of the decisions which fall to the independent farmer, but not to the dependent farmer, are decisions of *what* to produce; he is free, as the dependent farmer is not free, to switch from one crop to another, to change his rotation, or to change his mix between arable and pasture. To these we should add, under modern conditions, decisions about mechanization, about fertilizers and pesticides, and so on. In the case of the dependent farmer all these latter decisions are made, in principle at least, 'higher up'.

Tenant farmers, like peasant proprietors (or farmer-owners however described) will reckon on this classification as independent farmers; but the manager of a plantation, even a large plantation, will be a dependent farmer. The distinction is clear, I think, in principle, though qualifications will no doubt be necessary in particular cases. The tenant farmer's freedom of decision-making may be limited by the terms of his contract; even the freedom of the farmer-owner is limited, and may be considerably limited, by the law of the land. The plantation manager may have a considerable degree of freedom delegated to him. But we can grant these qualifications and still maintain that in general the distinction holds.

The independent farmer, if he has any external payments to make (rent or taxes or debt charges) must produce for the market; he must sell to the market more than he buys from it, by the amount of his external payments. The dependent farmer does not have this market dependence; since the decision of what he is to produce is made for him, it is the maker of that decision who must have the disposal of the produce. The separation of responsibility for the disposal of the product from responsibility for the 'when' decisions which cannot be separated from the farmer is a *defect* of dependent farming. It is a defect which is more important in some conditions than in others (and by improvements in methods of management it can be diminished); and it may well be outweighed by countervailing advantages. But in itself it is a defect; for the day-to-day administration of a farm, involving continual adjustment to uncontrollable or not easily controllable natural processes, is an activity which is not easy for an outsider to oversee. Independent farming's combination of responsibility for the day-to-day decisions, and for the longer-term decisions, and for the disposal of the product, is a merit. It is a merit which often outweighs the considerable disadvantages which must be set against it.[1]

For when the farm is defined as I have just defined it, there must be a limit to its size. The limit is more constricting in some sorts of agriculture than in others, but it always exists. Under independent farming the limit to the size of the farm is a limit to the size of the enterprise; under dependent farming the individual farm is no more than a part of the enterprise of which it is a member. Smallness of size *of the enterprise* is accordingly a characteristic of independent farming: not a universal characteristic, for conditions do exist in which the independent farm can grow to a size in which its smallness is

[1] One thinks of the characterization of the entrepreneur that is given by von Thünen; though it is meant to apply to industry, it is surely of his own experience in farming that he is thinking.

'When trade is bad and he is making losses, when his fortune and his reputation alike are at hazard, his mind is fixed on the avoidance of disaster; sleep deserts him on his bed.

It is otherwise with the salaried manager. When he has done his day's work and goes home in the evening, he sleeps sound, conscious of duty done.

But the sleepless nights of the entrepreneur are not unproductive.'

(*Der Isolierte Staat*, Part 2, Ch. 7. The useful translation by Father Dempsey, surprisingly entitled *The Frontier Wage*, Loyola University, Chicago 1960, does not always get the spirit of the original; so I have modified it a little.)

not much of a problem; but a characteristic that is very usual indeed.

Smallness of size of the enterprise implies, as a rule, lack of capital. There are two main reasons why the independent farmer requires capital. One, which is nowadays so important, is in order that he should be able to invest in farm machinery and to make other costly improvements; the other, which has always been important, is that he should have a reserve. Agricultural processes are inherently risky. The output that results, on a given piece of land, from a given application of labour, may sometimes be plentiful and sometimes miserable. The farmer who is producing for his own consumption is adversely affected by natural disasters; the farmer who is producing for the market is adversely affected by such disasters, but he is also affected adversely by an expansion of the output of those who compete with him. The inelasticity of demand for many agricultural products implies that when there is an abnormally good harvest, affecting all or most of the farmers who produce for a particular market, the latter effect will outweigh the former. Thus it is inevitable, in an unregulated market, that the value of the farmer's output will be very variable. In a year when the value of his output is low (either because of a low volume or because of a low price) he will be hard put to it to meet his outgoings; this will be so even though his farm, from a long-run point of view, is a perfectly viable concern.

There is a need for capital to meet such emergencies: a need which with the small independent farmer is notoriously acute. If he owns his land, and has not already borrowed against it, he may give it as security for borrowing. As we have seen, that can happen, but it is by no means reliable as a way out. For the condition in which the borrower is unable to repay is only too likely to be one in which the taking-over of the land is of no use to the lender. The land is then an uncertain security, so that the only borrowing which is open is in effect unsecured borrowing. The association, so often experienced, between independent farming and indebtedness to usurers needs no further explanation.

Independent farming (or, more strictly, small-scale independent farming) is thus in itself by no means a reliable
answer to the agrarian problem. It needs to be fortified by
arrangements for agricultural credit—from a source which is
not simply concerned with the short-term profit that may be
extracted from the making of loans to farmers individually,
but which is concerned with the long-term profitability of the
farmers who are its clients, as a group. The loans that are
made from such a source cannot be 'at arm's length'; whatever the formal terms, the substance must be something in the
nature of a partnership. Even the independent farmer must
sacrifice something of *financial* independence.

The support that he requires can be provided in various
ways: mainly nowadays through agricultural credit institutions and Land Banks, and through co-operatives. But it is by
no means ruled out that it may be provided, under appropriate conditions, through the private landlord. It is worth a
landlord's while, if he has sufficient capital and is looking to
his own long-run interest, to 'see his tenants through'.

It is, however, in the provision of the other kind of agricultural capital that the landlord–tenant system is more at
home. For land which has remained in the ownership of the
landlord, and is due to revert to his disposal on the expiry of a
lease, offers to him a very high degree of security in the making
of long-term improvements. He must, as before, have money
to invest (or must himself be able to raise it); and the technical opportunity of improving productivity by the long-term
investment of capital must of course be open. If these conditions are satisfied (as in the classical landlord–tenant system
of England they were rather generally) the landlord finds a
new function, entering with his tenants into a new kind of
partnership. His rent is no longer a payment for the 'original
and indestructible powers of the soil' as Ricardo called it
—a payment which even on commercial principles is so
difficult to justify; it becomes, at least in large measure, a
regular return upon a commercial investment.

But this again is only one way in which the need for long-
term capital may be met. Credit institutions that were pri-

marily designed for the other purpose may do something to combine it with this; while the State, which had previously taken over the landlord's old function as Protector, may take over this new function also. Through its modern control over the banking system, it can readily become a source of capital for agriculture, provided in the name of Development.

To have the State as partner, or provider of capital; to have it also as protector, not only in the old sense, but exercising monopoly powers on his behalf so as to protect him from the fluctuations of the market; when these services are provided for him, the problems of the 'independent' farmer, which have vexed him for so long, may appear to be solved. Yet how much, then, is left of his independence? It is by his political weight that he has attained this favoured position, and that could prove to be a wasting asset.

It is notorious that the technical improvements which have transformed the agriculture of so many countries in this century are diminishing the proportion of the population that is engaged in agriculture. What had been the chief of all economic occupations, is becoming a single 'industry' like the rest.[1] A further consequence of these same improvements has been a great increase in the size of the unit (measured at least in terms of output) that can conveniently be managed

---

[1] Perhaps it is not so generally realized how rapid the diminution has become. The following figures (derived from the current O.E.C.D. Labour Statistics) tell their own tale.

Percentage of occupied population occupied in agriculture

	1956	1966
U.K.	6·1	4·6
U.S.A.	9·9	5·5
Germany	16·9	10·8
France	25·9	17·6
Italy	32·7	23·8
Japan	38·5	24·2

There are many other countries which show a similar contraction.

While the contraction is proceeding, the pressure for agricultural protection is naturally very strong; but when it is completed, when the percentage settles down, as it seems likely to do, at not more than 10 per cent, even in non-food-importing countries, will the farmer be so powerful as a 'pressure group'? One must doubt it.

by the single farmer. So the farmer is less of a 'small man' than used to be the case, and is tending to be in less need of special assistance in obtaining capital. Yet another consequence (one would guess) is an increase in the relative advantage of dependent farming, large estates becoming easier to manage. The general drift of all these changes is for agriculture to become less unlike other industries than it has been in history, almost up to the present. That the State will continue to play a part in the organization of agriculture, in some way or other, cannot be doubted; but its agricultural policy may well come to be more like its policy towards other industries. It will then appear that you cannot give everyone privileges against everyone else.

VIII

THE LABOUR MARKET

To regard the formation of a labour market as a 'penetration', analogous to the penetration of the market system into agriculture, may seem at first sight to be a little far-fetched. I had better explain what I mean by it.

Labour, in the sense I am using it in this chapter, is not just 'work'. Each of the classes of people, whose activities we have been surveying, has its work. The peasant has his work, the administrator has his work, the merchant has his work; even the landlord, so long as he retains a positive function, has his work. The characteristic of the labourer, or worker in the narrower sense to which we have come, is that he *works for* someone else. He is (let us not be afraid to say it) a *servant*.

The Mercantile Economy has never been able to dispense with servants. But the relation of master and servant (including in that, when we come to it, the relation of a modern firm to its employees) is not, and never has been, a normal mercantile relation. As we should now be ready to recognize, it is much older than the Mercantile Economy. It is a piece of a Command system. That is where it belongs; it has never been at home in a mercantile system. It is the command system which is naturally hierarchical; which runs (and thinks) in terms of the relation of leader to follower, lord to vassal, master to servant; a relation based partly on force, but partly also upon its own variety of ethical sentiment, loyalty on the one side, responsibility on the other. The mercantile system is not hierarchical; buyer and seller are 'on a level'; why should one be master and one servant? The master–servant relation does not fit.

In the pre-mercantile economy (as illustrated by the lord-and-peasant system which we have been discussing) the servant (or whatever he was called) had a clear place. Not an exalted place, nor one in which he was safe from oppression; but one in which it was possible for him, at least in quiet times, to live a continuous life, consistent with his social needs, especially those concerned with the long process of upbringing children; a status which laid heavy obligations upon him, but in which he had some protection from his fellows, and even (as we have seen) from his lord, to set on the other side. The position is very different when labour is mercantilized, when labour has become an article of trade.

> There souls of men are bought and sold
> And milk fed infancy for gold
> And youth to slaughter houses led
> And beauty for a bit of bread[1]

These are feelings that must not be suppressed; they belong to the issue.

There are two ways in which labour may be an article of trade. Either the labourer may be sold outright, which is slavery; or his services only may be hired, which is wage-payment. The former may be regarded as a direct adaptation of the master–servant relation of the Command economy to mercantile conditions; it is only too obvious that in the translation that old relation is likely to lose what virtues it had. For there is no reason, on mercantile principles, why the slave should not be re-sold; if he is liable to be re-sold, the stability of the relation (and the sense of duty on both sides which is called forth by stability) is likely to be lost. The latter, it will certainly be claimed, is the more thoroughly mercantile arrangement; but the most perfectly mercantilized labour market is the market for casual labour, where the servant may be thrown off, and the master may be deserted, at almost any moment. If the labour market is formed in the image of a commodity market, that is what it is like.[2] A market for wage-

[1] Blake, Rossetti MS.
[2] It should (theoretically) be possible to make long-term contracts for the delivery of labour, just as long-term contracts are made, on occasion, for the

labour is not necessarily of this character, or not entirely of this character; but this is the direction in which mercantilization, as such, tends to move it.

I shall proceed, in this chapter, to examine both kinds of labour market. Each is of the greatest historical importance, and we shall find, when we consider them together, that they throw light on each other.

In the early days of the Mercantile Economy, as in ancient Greece, it was mainly the method of slavery that was used; later it has been mainly the other. It is easy to see why it was that mercantile labour began as slavery.

When the Mercantile Economy was growing up, on the edge of its command-customary predecessor, the easiest way for the merchant to get servants was to buy slaves—from some neighbouring lord or chieftain, who had prisoners of war to dispose of, or who could be induced, by a money payment, to go out and get them. They had to be brought from their homes to a new place; temporary hiring meant bearing the cost of returning them; it was easier to buy them outright.

Even within the institution of slavery, it is necessary to make distinctions. The catching of slaves has always been a brutal business; it must always be so, from the nature of the case. But in the treatment of the slave, once he has passed into the hands of the owner, who is to make use of him, there are many varieties.

A principal use of slaves, almost everywhere (excepting in some recent instances, to which we shall be coming), has been in domestic service. This has, on the whole, the reputation of being a mild form of slavery. It may be of no great importance to the servants of a household that they are legally slaves; since their master has to live with them (as a group if not necessarily individually) he will have a quieter life if he is considerate of them, winning their loyalty and even their

delivery of commodities. But, excepting in the form of apprenticeship contracts (which are commonly regarded, when considered from this point of view, as semi-slavery), they do not easily arise in a free labour market.

On apprenticeship, see below, pp. 139–40.

affection. This can be; and over the long ages and many countries in which slaves have been employed as domestic servants, a fairly harmonious relation of this character may well have been established more often than not. Harmony, however, implies no more than that the slave is treated no worse than he, or she, expects to be treated; when the customary moral standards are low, that may not mean much.[1]

In our early Mercantile Economy, merchants would be buying slaves in order to get servants; and when once a supply of slaves had been established, they would be ready to sell slaves, to whoever would buy them at a price which would give a profit. Landowners as well as merchants would be buying slaves. The large landowner, who could rely for service upon 'his' peasants and their children, might have little demand for the imported article; but if slaves were cheap enough there would be a demand for them much lower down the scale. In ancient Athens, we are told by Professor Andrewes,[2] 'a single family tilling a small plot of land would normally own slaves'. A slave or two, belonging to a small man, whether employed in domestic service or in agriculture, could as before be treated very much as a part of the family; so this again could be a mild form of slavery.

More strictly mercantile, and in the ancient world of quite special importance, is the employment of slaves in shops and workshops; the trader or independent craftsman (whom, it will be remembered, we are reckoning as a trader[3]) working alongside the slaves who are his assistants, and who are his property. This again is a personal relationship, and must often have been made more tolerable by the personal association. But the workshop (especially under slavery) would often be a sweatshop; for it is hard for the trader not to drive his assistants as he drives himself. If he does so (since they do not have his incentive) he is a tyrant.

[1] The sexual implications of domestic slavery are an aspect we must not omit to face. It is no accident that the power of one human being over another, which is inherent in slavery, should so often find expression in sexual subjugation. Words change their meanings with states of society; but concubine, over most of history, is a word for a slave.

2. A. Andrewes, *The Greeks*, p. 135.   [3] See above, pp. 28–9.

Each of these forms of 'small-scale' slavery has its dark side; but in each of them a possibility is open that is not quite so dark. For while the slave is in personal contact with his master, he retains his individuality. Because he retains his individuality, it is not excluded that he may earn what is in effect promotion; he may acquire responsibility. Even the domestic slave may be set over other slaves; the farm-labourer slave may find himself, on the death or illness of his master, in effective charge of the farm; the shop or workshop assistant may be entrusted with responsibilities of many kinds. It seems indeed to have been by no means uncommon (in Greece and in Rome) for a trader to retire, at the end of his working life, and to leave his business to be carried on by his slaves.[1]

'Small-scale' slavery, of which these relatively good things might be said, must surely have been the way in which mercantile slavery began; but having gone so far, it would go further. The darkest episodes in the history of mercantile slavery (putting aside, as before, the horrors of slave-catching, which always apply) are a matter of the large-scale employment of slaves; the employment of slaves in gangs, on plantations (such as the Roman latifundia, and the cotton and sugar plantations of America and the West Indies), in mines, and as galley-slaves on ships.

> I am acquainted with sad misery
> As the tanned galley-slave is with his oar

says the Duchess of Malfi, in a comparison that cuts both ways. The gang-slave is hardly a man; he is 'undifferentiated labour'.

---

[1] The legal complications which arose when that happened are interesting. Slaves who did business for their masters had to be able to enter into contracts; it was even necessary for them to be able, in some way, to hold property. Theoretically, it was still the case that the property 'owned' by the slave, like the slave himself, belonged to his master; but it was nevertheless necessary that he should be given some power of disposal over it, in order that he should be able to convey a title to it to the person to whom he sold it.

The ingenuity of Roman lawyers rose to the occasion. A special kind of property ('peculium') was devised, in order to make it possible for slaves to do business. (Crook, *Law and Life of Rome*, London 1967, pp. 188–91). Perhaps it should be said that when this point is reached, the slave is only a semi-slave.

Even here, however, there are distinctions. They are recognizable in the history, and there is an economic logic behind them.

To the slave-owner, operating a fairly large-scale enterprise with slave labour, the slave is an instrument of production, entering into his calculations in the same way as any other instrument of production; in the same way, that is, as a machine is regarded by a modern manufacturer. The profitability of the use of a machine depends upon the relation between its purchase price and the value of the net product that is expected from it; net product being gross product *less* maintenance. Maintenance, however, is not a fixed sum. There is always a choice between investing capital in the maintenance of the future productivity of existing assets, and investing it buying new ones; or putting it aside to buy new ones at an earlier date than would have been necessary if the other course had been followed. The lower the price of new machines, the more likely it is that frequent replacement will be preferred.

In a slave establishment, operating on strict business lines, the same principle applies. When slaves are cheap and easily obtainable, it will pay to keep the sums invested in their maintenance to a minimum; but when slaves are harder to get and more expensive, so that the loss of a slave, or his inability to work, is a serious matter, it will be profitable to undertake expenditure to diminish the risk of its occurrence. It is evident that in this latter case the treatment of the slave is likely to be better. It is to the advantage of the slave that the sums spent upon his maintenance should be as large as possible; for they are the nearest thing that he gets to a *wage*.[1]

[1] It is in accordance with this that the concession, sometimes made when prisoners of war were sold into slavery, of promising them their liberty after a period of years, was very doubtfully in their interest; for if their owner (or employer) could not expect to keep them when their term expired, the incentive to him to spend upon their maintenance was reduced. It is related that when the Royalist prisoners, taken at Colchester in 1648, after one of the most savage episodes of the English Civil War, were sold into slavery at Barbados 'for five years', few of them survived to get their liberty. (S. R. Gardiner, *Great Civil War*, London 1891, vol. 3, p. 464; *Commonwealth and Protectorate*, London 1894, vol. i, p. 351).

There is indeed a distinction, sufficiently recognizable in historical examples, between the kind of gang- or mass-slavery which occurs when slaves are cheap—when it pays to work them literally to death, and then to replace them on the market—and the appreciably milder kind which is found when replacement through the market is more difficult. When the loss of a slave is a serious matter to the owner, it pays to give some attention to his 'welfare'. Quite as important is the fact that it is profitable, in the same conditions, to maintain the supply of slaves by natural reproduction. It is profitable to the slave-owner, in the latter case but not in the former, for his slaves to have children.

One can therefore appreciate the force of the contention, often advanced by economists, that the abolition of the Slave Trade was more important, for the welfare of existing slaves, than the Abolition of Slavery itself. It is not simply that the Slave Trade, and the slave-catching which it was bound to involve, was so ghastly.

> As a shark and dogfish wait
> Under an Atlantic isle
> For the negro ship, whose freight
> Is the theme of their debate

Shelley's unforgettable summary of a hundred indictments.[1] The loss of slaves on the 'Middle Passage' was an inefficiency in the Slave Trade; but the more efficient the trade became, the lower would be the supply price of new slaves, and the worse the condition of the former slaves was likely to be. Only when the Slave Trade was cut off could the value of the slave

---

[1] One is however tempted to match it with the description, given by an English traveller at nearly the same date as Shelley's poem, of slave-catching in the Arab slave trade in the Western Sudan (supplying slaves across the Sahara to the Islamic Mediterranean):

'They rest for the night, two or three hours' ride from the village intended to be attacked; and after midnight, leaving their tents and camels with a small guard, they advance so as to arrive by day light; they then surround the place and, closing in, generally succeed in taking all the inhabitants ... At a convenient distance is placed a standard, round which are stationed men prepared to receive and bind the captives' (Captain G. F. Lyon, 1821; quoted in E. W. Bovill, *The Niger Explored*, Oxford 1968, p. 67, who adds 'A terrible aspect of these raids, not known to Lyon, was the slaughter of all unsaleable captives, the old and middle-aged of both sexes').

rise above the floor which it set. Only then (so the argument went) would the condition of the slave be substantially improved.

There is indeed some evidence that the condition of the slave, after the abolition of the trade, but before emancipation,[1] was moving towards something at first sight not unlike the condition of the peasant in a lord-and-peasant system. The 'domestic economy' of the 'estate slaves' in Jamaica, just before emancipation, has been described in the following terms:[2]

They had occupied cottages for which they paid no rent and given long labour for which they received no money wages, but their owners had at least provided the subsistence minima of food, clothing and household utensils. They had cultivated provisions and sometimes raised pigs, poultry and other live stock, on land for which they paid no rent. The products had been used as food for themselves and surpluses had been sold for money or bartered on local markets.[3] The money derived from such sales had been used to buy supplementary items of food, clothing and household goods, to contribute to the various dissenting missions to which the majority belonged; or simply hoarded in an attempt to accumulate enough to buy their freedom.

But my author continues—and it is this which marks the difference

Because they were so generally liable to be sold or transferred from one estate to another, slaves can have had little inducement to invest their money in goods which they could not easily carry with them if the occasion arose.

The peasant, in a typical lord-and-peasant system, was liable to be 'sold'; but only when the land to which he was attached was sold with him. Thus what was sold was not so much the peasant himself as the rights of lordship over him. The mark of commercial slavery, even at its best, is the possi-

[1] The Slave Trade was abolished, as far as British legislation could abolish it, in 1806; emancipation in British colonies followed in 1833. It was only in 1865 that slavery was abolished in the United States, by the Thirteenth Amendment to the American Constitution.

[2] Douglas Hall, *Free Jamaica, 1838–65 (an economic history)*, Yale 1959, p. 157. (1838 is the date at which the transitional provisions of the emancipation legislation expired).

[3] The local markets which still exist in Jamaica go back to the markets which the slaves ran on Sundays. 'Linstead Market' is a famous Calypso.

bility of individual re-sale. There is a world of difference between a system in which slaves can be sold individually, without reference to family attachments, or to any other social linkages which they may have formed; and one in which it is only the village, the whole social complex and the land that is attached to it which can be sold as a unit. The former is a social evil that is much greater than the latter. It is not only that the peasant can build up a protection from custom, which in the case of the slave must be largely absent. It is also that the slave, being subject to individual re-sale, though he may beget children, is inhibited from entering into a stable parental relation with them. Slavery, in almost every form, is an enemy of the family.[1]

I pass to the consideration of the 'free' labour market, the labour market of the second kind. We may best approach it by enquiring how it is that the one has given place to the other.

We must, for this purpose, go back beyond the abolition of negro slavery. That is a story which can well be told, in its main outline, in legal, moral, and political terms;[2] but the antecedent question—why it was that Europe, many centuries earlier, had gone over almost entirely to the free labour system —must have an answer that is mainly economic.[3] Ancient slavery was not rooted out, as negro slavery may be held to have been in the nineteenth century, by an upsurge of moral feeling. Though the centuries during which it declined were the centuries in which Europe became Christian, there is little evidence that the Church was greatly concerned with the

[1] The social consequences which follow are not easily eradicated. In the Jamaican census of 1950, 70 per cent of the population were reckoned as, at least nominally, 'illegitimate'.

[2] That it is right to tell it in these terms was denied by Eric Williams (now Prime Minister of Trinidad) in his celebrated book *Capitalism and Slavery*, North Carolina 1943). Most of Williams' thesis has however been refuted by Roger Anstey (*Economic History Review*, August 1968). All that remains is the unquestionable fact that abolitionists, being for the most part economic liberals, underestimated the defects of the free labour market.

[3] I have been greatly helped by the analysis of the decline of slavery in Europe in the paper of Marc Bloch already mentioned (*Cambridge Economic History of Europe*, vol. I, first edition, pp. 234–43, second edition, pp. 246–55).

question of slavery. It was concerned with the soul of the slave, but not with his status. The principal reason why free labour displaced slave labour was that in the conditions when the change occurred, free labour was cheaper.

One kind of labour may be cheaper than another, to the employer, because it is more efficient; but I do not think it was only (or even mainly) by that kind of cheapness that free labour displaced the slave. For the relative efficiency of free labour and slave labour is not as simple a matter as it looks at first. A free labourer, paid on piece work, will certainly tend to be more efficient than a slave, when the slave is given no such incentive; but when the work to be done is such that payment in relation to output is easy, there is really no reason why the slave should not be given a bonus, in some form or other. It is by no means clear that free labour, on time-work, is necessarily more efficient than slave labour. The free labourer, if he slacks, may be dismissed; but the slave, if he slacks, may be sold. When the issue is put between the employment of slaves, on a fairly small scale, and the employment of free labour on a similar scale—a scale that is small enough for individual performance to be recognized by the employer (and that, at the stage we are considering, must in most cases have been the practical issue)—it is by no means clear that there is any considerable difference.

Assume that efficiency is equal. The question is then of the cost of labour, on the one method and on the other, *per unit of time*. The cost of slave labour to the slave owner, per unit of time, consists of maintenance plus interest (and depreciation) on capital cost. Maintenance is compounded of short-term maintenance (which has to be met in any case) and longer-term maintenance (directed towards future production capacity), which (as we have seen) can to some extent be avoided when capital cost is low, but can be substituted for capital cost when the latter is higher. The cost per period must therefore be greater than short-term maintenance for the period; the difference consisting either of interest and depreciation on capital cost (which is the main element when reliance is placed upon the market to maintain the supply of slaves) or of longer-term maintenance (which may be the principal element if replacement through the market is expensive, or less readily available). Whichever way is adopted, the difference will be greater when slaves are scarce than when they are abundant. It is a difference which cannot fall to zero; since if it did the supply of slaves would dry up.

What is the corresponding calculation in the case of free labour? The employer of free labour, on a free market, has no responsibility for his employee beyond the period for which the contract of employment runs; thus the wage which he has to pay is the whole of the cost, and that is simply determined by what the worker is willing to accept, which in turn is a matter of the availability of alternative opportunities. If labour is scarce, the wage (as a market price) may rise very high; but if labour is abundant it can fall very low, to something which corresponds to no more than the maintenance of the slave—even to the short-period, or nearly short-period maintenance of the slave. In each case, therefore, the cost of labour is a matter of the scarcity or abundance of labour, expressed as a supply price. There is no inevitability about the supply price of the one sort of labour being higher or lower than the other. If slave labour is plentiful, it will drive out free labour; but if free labour is relatively plentiful, it will drive out slavery. They are competing sources; when both are used the availability of one affects the value (wage or capital value) of the other.

Most of what happened can, I believe, be explained in these terms: provided that we add the point (a rather obvious point, when one thinks of it) that there is usually[1] a certain reluctance to make slaves of those who are recognized as belonging, in some way or another, to one's own people. This is partly a matter of morals—not necessarily very elevated morals; but it has a practical basis from which it probably has its origin, and which (in the rough world with

---

[1] Usually, for we have to take account of the use of enslavement as a punishment, for crime or insolvency. This has not infrequently been practised, in the absence of a system of prisons; but it could hardly be the basis of a regular dependence upon slavery.

which we are here concerned) makes it more dependable. It
is not easy to enforce a system of slavery unless the slave is
distinguishable by some mark that is readily recognizable. It
may be his appearance (that is where colour comes in, but
appearance can be recognized in other ways than by colour);
it may be—and originally I expect it mainly was—his
speech.

Greeks, as late as the time of the Peloponnesian War, had
no compunction about enslaving Greeks; but the variety of
dialects made Greeks from different parts rather readily
recognizable. Romans, a couple of centuries later, had no
compunction about enslaving Greeks, or any other of the
peoples who had come into their power; it does indeed seem
likely that it was in the second century b.c., when Rome was
conquering the Mediterranean lands, that the greatest multitudes of slaves were thrown upon the market. One would
certainly guess that it would have been at this stage that the
value of the slave was lowest, his condition worst, and the
destructive force of his competition, upon what remained of
the free market, at its maximum. All the indications are that
this was a time of great social stress.[1] Afterwards, however, in
the quieter times which followed the settlements by Caesar
and Augustus, though slavery persisted, the sources from
which such multitudes of slaves could be collected are less
easy to perceive. We should therefore expect both that the
condition of the slaves would be improved, and that the labour
force would come to consist to a larger extent of free labour
and less of slaves.

This is only a hypothesis; but it would make sense. Roman
legislation begins, even before the Empire is christianized, to
give the slave some rudimentary protection;[2] law can hardly
do more than enforce 'good current practice'; the presumption is that standards were in fact improving. And though
Christianity did not suppress slavery, it did encourage the
view that Christians (orthodox Christians, or established

---

[1] The most obvious indications are the agitations of the Gracchi, and the slave
revolts (Spartacus).

[2] *Cambridge Mediaeval History*, vol. 2, p. 62.

Christians) should not be taken and made slaves. The range of the people who were 'one's own people' in the sense above described was accordingly widened.

Slavery did not disappear; slaves are still provided for in the code of Justinian (sixth century A.D.); there was slave-trading and slave-raiding in western Europe for centuries after that. But it was mainly directed against non-Christian and semi-Christian peoples; and there were not many such who were open to be raided. Anglo-Saxons[1] and Germans until they were christianized; Slavs (who gave their name to the *slave*) until they too were christianized; but who else? The main potential source of slaves, to the south and east, was blocked by the military power of Islam.[2]

Thus it was that at the time of the economic expansion of the early Middle Ages (the 'second city-state phase' of our former analysis) slaves were scarce and expensive; if a source of free labour could be found, it was likely to undercut. And that, I suggest, is what happened. The Mercantile Economy of western Europe, in the Middle Ages, was insulated from a source of slaves; and by the time that the sea-route to Africa was opened up, in the fifteenth century, the free labour system was established.

Once a free labour system is established, it is likely to be cheaper. The slave must be brought to the market, so that the cost of bringing him to the market (or some substitute for it) is a component part of his price. The free labourer does not have to be brought; he brings himself. But why should he bring himself if the earnings that he gets for his trouble are so low that he can undercut the slave? Surely the answer is that *sometimes* they are not so low.

The Mercantile Economy offers opportunities, opportunities

[1] The 'non angli, sed angeli' of Pope Gregory.

[2] Moslems, like Christians, were reluctant to enslave those whom they recognized to be their fellows; but the establishment of the Moslem Empire, being a military conquest like the establishment of the Roman, provided them at first with an ample supply. Even later, they had access to sources of slaves, not only in Africa, but also in Asia and in Europe, which were denied during the Middle Ages to the peoples of Europe.

for rising. The movement from the country to the town (for that is the chief part of what is involved) is motivated by the possibility, held out by the town, of considerable or even dazzling advancement; an opportunity held out to all, though in fact it is only a few of those who move who will achieve it. The call of Bow Bells to Dick Whittington—'Lord Mayor of London'! In their sound we have a symbol of the enchantment which called into being the *urban proletariat*.[1]

Population pressure, of course, has something to do with it. I make no question that the flow to the town will be greater when the pressure on the land is greater than when it is less. It is now believed that in the early Middle Ages (eleventh to thirteenth centuries) there was a rapid increase in population over most of western Europe; this should certainly have helped to get the movement started. Even under a lord-and-peasant system, when population is increasing, there will be little objection if those for whom a place cannot readily be found just go away.[2] But it is not necessary that there should be population pressure. It is perfectly possible that there may be a persistence of *proletarian equilibrium*, even though there is no great land shortage, and even though the town population and the country population, taken separately, are each remaining stationary.

This can happen if the country population is more than reproducing itself, while the town population is less than reproducing itself—the excess population in the country moving to the town, so as to keep the number in the town, and the number who remain in the country, substantially unaltered. Some of those who move will do well, moving into the ranks of the merchant class, at higher or lower levels, replacing the failures which the merchant class will itself breed in every generation. But most of those who move will fail to make the grade, drifting into casual employment and semi-employment,

---

[1] There was a real Sir Richard Whittington, Lord Mayor of London in the early fifteenth century; but he was not a 'poor boy who made good'. For the origins of the legend (more significant for my purpose than fact) see the article on Whittington in the *D.N.B.*

[2] See above, p. 113.

half workers and half beggars; a condition in which they are unable (even less able than the slave) to maintain a family life, so that the urban proletariat which they form will diminish over the generations if it is not reinforced by newcomers, the products themselves of the same process. This, of course, is only a 'model'; but it is a model which, when adjusted in each case for differences in geography and other such influences, seems to fit the condition of many great cities, over many centuries, with a free labour market.[1]

Now it will be noticed that an essential condition for the maintenance of this *proletarian equilibrium* is that those who are disappointed are unable to go back. The more easily they can go back, the higher will be the supply price of labour in the town; the more likely, therefore, that the town will be in a condition of labour scarcity, not labour abundance. In most cases, surely, it will not be easy to go back; the immigrant has given up his place in the country, and it will not be kept for him. Nevertheless there is one important case in which it is easy. This is the case of a new country, in which land is to be had for the taking; land which is good enough for a farmer, or squatter, to make a living on it. When this condition is satisfied, as it was, almost from the first, in the settlement of North America, urban wages are bound to respond. The urban worker has to be paid a high wage—what would elsewhere be regarded as an extraordinarily high wage—even for unskilled labour; for if he was not paid a high wage he would go away. Wages in America have in fact been higher than wages in Europe, almost from the time of the first settlements.

Here at least we seem to have a case in which the free market fulfils its promise and provides, even for Labour, an 'Allround Advantage'. But again there is a qualification—a formidable qualification. For it was a consequence of this

---

[1] Blake again permits one to summarize ('London' in *Songs of Experience*)

> But most through midnight streets I hear
> How the youthful Harlot's curse
> Blasts the new born infant's tear
> And blights with plagues the marriage hearse

It is the counterpoint to the sound of Bow Bells.

special condition that the slave system became, once again, cheaper than the free labour system. The same discoveries which were to open up the land of America had begun by giving access to a source of slaves in Africa. There was no demand for slaves in Europe, but there was in America. So it came about that at so late a stage in the evolution of the Mercantile Economy, there was a relapse into slavery.[1]

Is there not another, more regular, case in which the Mercantile Economy should fulfil its promise? Our proletarian equilibrium has been a *stationary* equilibrium, which could maintain itself, with its parts numerically unchanged, from year to year and from generation to generation. What happens if we superpose upon it, as we are surely entitled to do, a *growth* of the Mercantile Economy?

Even in the pre-industrial revolution conditions (with which in this chapter I am solely concerned) a growth in trade, including handicraft industry in trade, should surely imply an increase in the demand for labour. If this increase continues, and is not matched by an increase in supply, from rising population or accelerated influx from the 'country', must not the time come when the surplus of labour is absorbed, so that there is a general rise in wages? This is what, in terms of modern economics, we should expect; with sufficient expansion labour abundance should give place to labour scarcity.

One's impression is, nevertheless, that in pre-industrial conditions this rarely happened. Part of the explanation must be that the expansion that occurred was so limited and so localized. The agricultural sector of the economy was so vast; the opportunities for commercial employment, even when rising, were still so small. We are acquainted with this kind of situation in the development of 'underdeveloped' countries in our own day; there can be little doubt that the analogy

[1] The substitution of negro slave labour for free white labour is directly traceable in the seventeenth-century history of the Eastern Caribbean. Of course there was a change of crop (from tobacco to sugar); one must, however, conclude that if it had not been for the availability of the cheap slave labour (cheap in these particular conditions) sugar production could not have developed.

holds. But there is another reason for the failure to absorb which is also suggested by that analogy.

We should not allow ourselves to think of the labour force, in the 'town', as being homogeneous. It is inevitable, in a free labour market, that some kinds of labour should be scarcer than others, and that the scarcer labour should command higher wages. But not only higher wages; for the undependability and unpredictability of a labour market which approaches the character of a commodity market bear hard on the worker; as soon as he can afford it, he will be willing (or will often be willing) to sacrifice something in wages for the sake of security. Thus the higher grades of labour will have more security, more regular employment, as well as higher wages. There are highest grades, where the employee can make himself individually so valuable to his employer that he can be sure to have 'work found for him' even if at the moment he should not be so urgently wanted; and there are middle grades, which by organization (the gilds and apprenticeship arrangements which have come up in so many times and places) can win for themselves some measure of security. The lowest grades, whom I am calling the urban proletariat, have (at the stage we are considering) neither security nor high wages.

Most of the labour that comes in is bound to be, from the point of view of urban employment, low-grade labour. But a general expansion of demand, from whatever source it comes, is likely to be spread, in proportions that will vary from one occasion to another, over all grades. If it were the case that movement from one grade to another were easy, employment could expand in each grade by movement up the scale; there would then be room, if only at the bottom, for the low-grade labour to be absorbed. But in fact the grades impose obstacles to movement, obstacles which can be worn down, but which are very resistant. A general increase in the demand for labour will therefore exhaust itself, in part, in a relative rise of wages in the higher grades—or in the taking by those grades of some equivalent advantage. This does indeed give an incentive for the substitution of higher grade labour by lower grade labour, and some of that there may well be; the more there is, the more of the demand will flow over to the lower grade labour. But neither along this route, nor along the other, is the way easy. The general effect of the grading (I prefer to use a less emotive and more general expression than 'class structure') is that the expansion of demand for the lower grade labour, which might in the end have absorbed the urban proletariat, is damped down.

The passage from one grade to another is largely a matter of training; and training is a process with which the free labour market does not readily cope. Education is a service which the market will provide for those who are willing to pay for it; but education, provided in that way, simply acts as a means by which those who are in the higher grades hand on their privileges to their children. (The tendency of an educational system to work in that manner had of course been tempered, even before the days of State education, by charitable endowments.) Training 'on the job' to which one might have supposed that access would be easier, shares in fact, at least to some extent, the same defect.

On the principles of the free market, the trainee (whose future productive capacity is being increased) is drawing an advantage for which he should pay; or, what comes to the same thing, he should be willing to accept a wage which is less than the wage he could get elsewhere without getting this advantage. But this, when unskilled wages are low, he cannot do. He requires to borrow in order to pay for productive investment in his capacity; but he does not have the credit with which to borrow. In the contract of apprenticeship, the imperfect solution to this dilemma which has been widely adopted, he borrows from his employer, giving himself into bondage as the only security he can offer. He is overpaid at the beginning of his time, and underpaid at the end. Thus it is to the interest of the employer to spread out the apprenticeship in order to have a longer period in which to recoup himself—thus in effect charging a high, even a usurious, rate of interest. The apprentice who is bound to his master in this manner is in a position not entirely different from that of the slave who is to be given his liberty at a fixed date; only if his master expects to want to keep him, and to be able to keep him when his time is up, is he safe from exploitation. Contracts of 'apprenticeship' in which the main advantage accrues to the employer, leaving very little to the apprentice who has been 'trained', are only too familiar. They are what is likely to occur when the contract is simply treated as a means of buying and selling labour, having no element of social responsibility in it. In the more respectable systems of apprenticeship, there is indeed such an element; but it is more easily aroused when master and apprentice have some social linkage in common. And that is likely to mean that the apprenticeship system, like the education system, is acting as a means of preserving the privileged position of the higher grades.

How much of this has been altered, or is on the way to being altered, by the Industrial Revolution of the last 200 years, we shall see in the next chapter.

IX

THE INDUSTRIAL REVOLUTION

THE Industrial Revolution is the Rise of Modern Industry,[1] not the rise of industry as such; but what is Modern Industry? What is the essential mark by which we are to distinguish it from 'ancient' industry, the handicraft industry which is coeval with the Market itself? Technologically, of course, there are various answers; some of them, as we go on, we shall find to be of help. But what we mainly need, for our purpose, is an economic answer.

Handicraft industry, I have insisted,[2] is barely distinguishable economically from trade. The artisan who produces for the market is a trader; he buys to sell again, so he must be a trader. What he sells is in a different form from what he buys, while the sales of the pure trader are physically in the same form; that is all the difference. As for 'mixing his labour' with the materials on which he works, the trader also is 'mixing his labour' (and that of the clerks and warehousemen whom he employs) in order to sell something which is of greater value than what he buys—or greater value because it is available at a place or at a time which is of more use to his customer. There is, in economic terms, an exact correspondence.

Though philosophers (and sometimes even economists) have found it hard to admit the correspondence, in practical life it is admitted. The formal statement of the economic activities of a business is to be found in its accounts. There is complete

<hr>

[1] The synonym that was used by J. L. and Barbara Hammond in the title of one of their books (London 1925).
[2] Above, p. 28.

continuity between the form of accounts which is appropriate for a firm that is engaged in manufacture, and that which is appropriate for a firm that is engaged in trade. Just the same items appear in both. It may indeed be said that in all those aspects of its activity which appear in its accounts, the manufacturing firm is treated, and treats itself, as a trader.

There is, however, one respect in which the correspondence is nowadays less than complete; this, I am going to suggest, is a clue to the distinction between the two kinds of industry, for which we are looking. The capital of a merchant is, mainly, working or circulating capital—capital that is *turned over*. (The use of the term *turnover* in relation to manufacturing, where it does not at all so obviously apply, is an example of the way the manufacturing firm still thinks of itself as a trader.) A particular merchant may indeed employ some fixed capital, an office, a warehouse, a shop or a ship; but these are no more than containers for the stock of goods on which his business centres. Any fixed capital that he uses is essentially peripheral.

As long as industry remained at the handicraft stage, the position of the craftsman or artisan was not so very different. He did indeed have tools, but the tools which he used were not usually very valuable; the turnover of his materials was the centre of his business. (This, it will be noticed, is a condition which exactly fits the 'domestic system', so commonly employed, in which this essential capital is advanced to artisans by merchant-capitalists; the artisan has his tools, but they are not a major part of the capital employed.) It is at the point when fixed capital moves, or begins to move, into the central position that the 'revolution' occurs.

In the days before Modern Industry, the only fixed capital goods that were being used, and which absorbed in their production any considerable quantity of resources, were buildings and vehicles (especially ships). Buildings, however, were chiefly consumers' goods, not producers' goods; and vehicles, even if they were producers' goods, were ancillary to trade, not to manufacture. What happened in the Industrial Revolution, the late eighteenth-century Industrial Revolution, is that the range of fixed capital goods that were used in production, otherwise than in trade, began noticeably to increase. It was not a single increase, that was over and done with in a single phase; the increase has continued. It is this, not simply an increase in capital accumulation, but an increase in the *range and variety* of the fixed capital goods in which investment was embodied, which I maintain to be the correct economic definition of the change we are considering.

Industrialization, so defined, is a continuation of the process of mercantile development which we have examined in earlier chapters; and it is tempting to analyse it in similar terms. Northern Europe, where the revolution first occurred, was at the peak (if it had not been for these developments, it might have been past the peak) of a mercantile expansion, similar in many ways to those which we previously discussed in our analysis of the First Phase;[1] an expansion led first by Holland, then by England, nation states, but nation states that had much in common with the city states that had led the previous expansions. (It is remarkable how much of what I said about the city state will apply to the seventeenth-century Dutch republic. The Dutch heartland was defensible, in just the same way and for the same reasons that Venice was defensible. From that secure base they carried their colonies, their mercantile colonies, to regions that the Athenians and Venetians had never known, to the very ends of the earth.[2] The English case, after all, is not so very dissimilar.)

Thus there was a trade network already in existence, in active existence. Like its predecessors, it would be endeavouring to expand; like them, it could only maintain expansion by the continual discovery of new opportunities. The expansion of trade, developing the opportunities offered by geographical exploration, had long sufficed; but there is evidence that these opportunities, which in the early seventeenth century had been amply sufficient, were in the

[1] Chapter IV above.
[2] A rather moving example of a Dutch mercantile colony, with its fortifications largely intact, can still be seen by the visitor at Galle, on the south coast of Ceylon.

eighteenth closing up.[1] It may well be that the fundamental reason for this is that Europe was not well situated to be the centre of a carrying trade between extra-European areas; the slave trade between Africa and America, and the opium trade between India and China, being exceptions that only too obviously prove the rule. Thus if trade were to continue to grow, it was necessary that Europe itself should provide the exports—which is what, in the nineteenth century, it so abundantly did. One can therefore see an incentive for a change in direction. Something like this had happened before —in the development of the ceramics trade of Athens, and of the woollen industry of Florence; a stimulus to industrial development, from this cause, would not have been surprising. But why should it have been anything more than old-style industry? Why should the development have taken the form of investment in fixed capital?

A possible answer, following the same line of thought, is to be found in the financial development which (as we have seen)[2] had been occurring at the same time, at more or less the right time. It is not simply that rates of interest had fallen (as they had). What is more important is the greater availability of funds, of which the fall in interest was a symptom, but no more than a symptom. Circulating capital is continually *turned over;* it is continually coming back for reinvestment. But fixed capital is *sunk;* it is embodied in a particular form, from which it can only gradually, at the best, be released. In order that people should be willing, in an uncertain world, to *sink* large amounts of capital, they must either themselves be in possession of other resources, which they hold in a more liquid form, so that they can be quickly realized to meet emergencies; or they must be confident of being able to borrow—and that means borrowing from someone else (it may be a bank) who is able to borrow, or who has liquid funds. In the end, it is the availability of liquid funds which is

[1] It has often been observed that the closure of Japan, about 1650, and semi-closure of China at about the same date, put an end to hopes of expansion of trade with these important parts of the world.

[2] Above, pp. 79, 94.

crucial. This condition was satisfied in England (as in Holland and even in France) by the first half of the eighteenth century. Already, then, there were financial markets, on which a variety of securities could readily be sold.[1] The liquid asset was there, as it would not have been even a few years earlier. (This no doubt was itself a major reason why rates of interest came down.)

Part of what happened can probably be explained in these strictly economic terms; but they leave one dissatisfied. Surely there is something more. If one considers, not just the introduction of the early spinning machinery into the textile industries (operated, as at first it was, by the water-wheels that had been used for centuries), but Modern Industry as a whole, the other element is at once apparent. It is not just the discovery of new sources of power. It is science. It has always been true that the economy grows by the exploitation of new opportunities for investment, opportunities that are revealed by a process of exploration, by advancement of knowledge; but while in the former phase the exploration was mainly geographical, in the latter it has been scientific exploration of the physical world in a much wider sense. It is science, especially physical science, which has opened up such seemingly illimitable prospects for industry. This is a connection which, as time has gone on, has become increasingly apparent. It is less obvious at the start, but one does not have to go far beyond the start before one finds it.

Take the case, the very central case, of the steam-engine. No one could look for a steam-engine until he possessed some rudimentary knowledge of the relations of heat and pressure;

[1] Surely it is significant when we find Gay writing to Swift (April 1731): 'The day before I left London I gave orders for buying two South Sea or India bills for you which carry four per cent and are as easily turned into ready money as bank bills.' For financiers in general there were many other forms of liquid asset. (See the account of the evolution of financial markets in P. G. M. Dickson, *The Financial Revolution in England*, London 1967.)

It is commonly supposed that the collapse of the Law 'System' (1720) set back the corresponding development in France for many years. Yet in the correspondence of Voltaire with his agent (the abbé Moussinot) during the 1730s we find evidence of quite active financial dealings.

knowledge which in the eighteenth century was generally available, but had only been made available by the work of physicists about 1660. It was indeed a hundred years after that before a steam-engine, which realized more than a very small part of the potentialities of the invention, could be constructed. The obstacle was technical; how was an engine to be constructed which was strong enough to stand up to high pressures, and whose *moving* parts would fit? There were separate skills, already in existence, which went some way to meet these requirements. There were gunsmiths who dealt in resistance to pressures; and there were clockmakers and watchmakers who had mastered the art of making (on a small scale) moving fitting parts.[1] But how were these two exceedingly different techniques to be brought together? Almost everything which was right in the one was wrong in the other. It is not surprising that it took so long to do it, even after science had set the problem. Could it have been done, one wonders, if science had not been setting at the same time a whole range of other problems, which offered similar challenges to the technicians? The progress of science required scientific instruments, precision instruments of new kinds, which must have given a similar impulse to cross-fertilization. We note that James Watt, at the time when he made his invention of the condenser, that turning-point in the evolution of the steam-engine, was 'Mathematical Instrument Maker' to Glasgow University.[2]

This, however, was no more than the beginning; as time went on, the reliance upon the old crafts, or what remained of the old crafts, quite sensibly diminished. The first generation of machines were made by hand, with some assistance from water power; they were expensive, because of the scarcity of the highly skilled labour needed to construct them, and they were not very accurate, because of their continued reliance

[1] The mechanical clock goes back to the fourteenth (possibly even the thirteenth) century. The early history of mechanism, and of instruments (such as lathes) for making mechanisms, has chiefly to be told in terms of the manufacture of clocks (*History of Technology*, Oxford 1954–8, vol. 3, pp. 648 ff.).

[2] He was appointed in 1757 (ibid., vol. 4, p. 181).

upon this human element.[1] Cost was reduced, and accuracy improved, in the second generation—the machines that were made by machines. This is well explained by the author of the chapter on machine-tools in the *History of Technology*:[2]

Machine-tools make it possible to work metal objects of great size and to shape metals with an accuracy unattainable by hand. Moreover, the high speed of working with machine tools makes commercially practicable processes which, even if mechanically possible, cannot be performed economically by hand. . . . The invention and development of machine-tools was an essential part of the industrial revolution.

It may indeed be that we should be right to recognize it as *the* essential part. One has a feeling that our view of what happened is pulled out of shape by that early textile 'machinery': an episode which must be granted to be of major importance in the economic history of England, but which when more widely considered is revealed to be something of a sideline. Or perhaps one should say that it fits better as an appendage to the evolution of the 'old' industry than in the way it is usually presented as the beginning of the new. Certainly it marked a turn to fixed capital investment, though fixed capital investment that was not yet upon any great scale. The greater mobility of capital was thus a condition for it, but not (so far) much else. Would it have been impossible, if capital could have been raised (and it may be that even that would not have been a major difficulty), and if the regular water power of Lancashire had been available, for something very like it to have occurred (say) in fifteenth-century Florence? There is continuity between the *eighteenth*-century development of Lancashire and the West Riding and the things we have been surveying in the pre-industrial revolution world.

There might have been no Crompton and Arkwright, and still there could have been an Industrial Revolution; in its

[1] The 'accuracy' that was attainable at this stage is exemplified by Boulton's tribute (in 1776) to Wilkinson, who for several years had been boring the cylinders for Boulton and Watt's engines:
'Wilkinson hath bored us several cylinders almost without error; that of 50 inches diameter for Bentley and Co. doth not err the thickness of an old shilling in no part' (quoted ibid., vol. 4, p. 422). Wilkinson was using a water-wheel to drive his boring-machine.   [2] K. R. Gilbert (ibid., vol. 4, p. 417).

later stages it would have been much the same. The impact of science, stimulating the technicians, developing new sources of power, using power to create more than human accuracy, reducing the cost of machines until they were available for a multitude of purposes; this surely is the essential novelty, the essential revolution, working so vast a transformation because it can be repeated, one might almost say it repeats itself over and over again. It is a switch to fixed capital; but it only becomes a major switch to fixed capital at the point when this development has made the new fixed capital goods quite reasonably cheap.[1]

Now at last we are in a position to tackle the question that was left over at the end of the last chapter, and to which this chapter is leading up—the question of the impact of industrialization on the labour market. The effect of the English Industrial Revolution on the real wage of labour is a question which historians have long been discussing—with results that even now give no very decisive answer. It is fortunately unnecessary for me to enter upon these controversies; for they hardly touch on what, from my viewpoint, is the essential issue. There is no doubt at all that industrialism, in the end, has been highly favourable to the real wage of labour. Real wages have risen enormously, in all industrialized countries, over the last century; and it is surely evident that without the increase in productive power that is due to industrialization the rise in real wages could not possibly have occurred. The important question is why it was so long delayed. There is no doubt at all that it was delayed; whether there was a small rise, or an actual fall, in the general level of real wages in England between (say) 1780 and 1840 leaves that issue untouched. It is the lag of wages behind industrialization which is the thing that has to be explained.

[1] It was reported, as late as 1807, that 'the expense of machinery renders a steam-engine somewhat more than half as expensive as the number of horses for which it is substituted' (T. Young, *Lectures on Natural Philosophy*, quoted *History of Technology*, vol. 4, p. 164). Steam-power cannot then have won much on water-power. Even in 1835 'Lancashire and the West Riding of Yorkshire had 1369 steam-engines and 866 water-wheels' (ibid., p. 166).

Part of the explanation, in view of what I have said about the previous condition of the labour market, is easy enough. If we start from a condition in which labour is in abundant supply (and this, for the reasons stated, I believe to have been the usual condition of the English labour market in the eighteenth century), we should not expect to find that real wages would rise significantly until the surplus of labour had been removed. It is not surprising that it took a long time before this happened. Population, we know, was increasing rapidly; there was little opportunity for the absorption of additional labour into agriculture; so the supply of labour to industry, and to other urban occupations, was increasing very rapidly indeed. The demand for labour had to grow, for some appreciable time, at a greater rate than this growth in supply, before the surplus of labour could be absorbed.

Now what would be the effect of the new opportunities for fixed capital investment on the demand for labour? This is by no means a simple question; it is one to which economists (even the greatest economists) have given divergent answers. I think it turns out that this is not surprising (or disgraceful). There are several forces at work; sometimes one is dominant, sometimes another.

There is, of course, no question at all that machines do, very often, displace labour. It may be worth while to quote an outstanding (and very well authenticated) example from the early nineteenth century—Maudslay's block-making machinery, introduced into Portsmouth dockyard in 1801, by which 'ten unskilled men did the work of 110 skilled men'.[1] No wonder there were Luddites! Economists have throughout been aware of these facts, but they could always be dismissed as consequences of labour immobility. New techniques are bound to diminish the demands for some sorts of labour, and to increase the demands for others; but what is the balance? What is the net effect on the demand for labour as a whole?

A simple application of Keynesian analysis would fix attention on the rise in the 'marginal efficiency of capital'

[1] *History of Technology*, vol. 4, p. 427.

which is implied (is undoubtedly implied) in the 'inventions'. This, in the Keynesian model, would be favourable, on balance, to an increase in employment; that is to say, it would increase the demand for labour. There is indeed no question that this is the effect which we should expect *in the first phase*. While the machines (and other fixed capital goods, such as railways) are being built, there will be a tendency towards an expansion of credit, so that the demand for labour, in money terms, will rise. But it is after the machines have been built that they will, on the other view, displace labour. The Keynesian theory, taken in this way, is no more (and claims to be no more) than a short-period theory; it gives no guidance, or at least no direct guidance, on what is to be expected over the span of a couple of generations, the point which is here in question.

There is however a long-period theory, due originally to the 'classical' economists, Adam Smith and his followers, the economists of the time of which I am writing; it does direct itself at the issue with which we are concerned, and it would seem at first sight to give a similarly optimistic answer. If one looks across the booms and slumps, the expansions and contractions of credit, and fixed one's attention on the *trend*, it is the demand for labour at a given rate of *real* wages which becomes the essential issue. It is plausible to argue that this will expand more rapidly the faster is the general growth of the economy; that the economy cannot grow without capital investment; that from the long-period point of view discrepancies between saving and investment can be neglected, so that saving and investment are the same; and that therefore the rate of growth depends upon the rate of saving. If one adds the assumption (valid enough in many times and places, and surely valid for industrial revolution England) that profits are the main source of saving, it becomes likely that there will be more saving the higher are profits. 'Inventions' will not be adopted unless they raise profits; higher profits means more saving; a higher rate of saving means a higher rate of growth for the economy as a whole; and this, at least on the average over a fairly long period, and on the average over labour as a whole, should imply a more rapid growth in the demand for labour.

As we shall see, this is indeed a part of the truth; but it is not the whole truth. It was already perceived by the greatest of the classical economists that it was not. I do not think that Ricardo, in the first edition of his *Principles* (1817), goes any deeper (so far as this particular issue is concerned) than what has just been summarized. It was the optimistic conclusion which apparently results from this that was seized upon by his popularizers, the prophets of the New Capitalism; it was what suited them, and it was of course what they took. But Ricardo had candour and courage; he followed his reasoning where it led him, not just where he (or his friends) wanted it to go. In the last edition of his book that was published in his lifetime (1820), he added a chapter 'On Machinery', much less agreeable to his followers, which goes far to supply what was lacking.

It is not the whole capital employed in industry, but only the circulating capital part of it, which is strongly correlated with the demand for labour from industry (still at a constant level of real wages).[1] So long as the proportion of fixed to

[1] This is the doctrine that was later labelled by J. S. Mill the 'Wage Fund'— a striking expression but one which falls short of what is, or should be, intended. (Mill, as is well known, 'recanted the Wage Fund' at the end of his life; this I fear is evidence that he had never really understood it.) Circulating capital is not a *wage fund*; it is the goods in process (including normal stocks of materials, of half-finished and of finished goods) which are needed, in a productive process of any kind, to 'keep the wheels of industry turning round'. If one imitates the normal business practice of not taking a profit until goods are actually sold, and if one neglects the complication due to vertical disintegration of the same process into different firms, the value of the circulating capital reduces (approximately) to that of the labour embodied. There is no strict proportionality between this value, as it is at some particular time, and the value of the flow of labour being currently applied (even when one is abstracting from short-run fluctuations) but there is a good approximate proportionality. This, I believe, is what Ricardo meant; but Mill did not quite grasp the point.

When Ricardo died (in 1823) at the age of fifty-one, Mill was only seventeen. He was the son of Ricardo's closest friend. If Ricardo had lived, even another five years, he would have *tutored* Mill. By 1829 (which appears to be the date of the best of his *Unsettled Questions*) Mill was at the top of his form, doing his best work in economics. What could not those two have achieved if they had been able, even for a little, to work together? Each of them had courage and candour; and Mill, so much better than Ricardo, could explain.

circulating capital remains constant, this of course does not matter; the growth rate of each will be the same, and will be the same as the growth rate of the capital stock as a whole. It will then be true that anything which increases the growth rate of the capital stock as a whole will be inclined to increase the rate of growth of the demand for labour. But this was not the problem as Ricardo (rightly I think) came to see it. If there is a switch to fixed capital, and *as a result of that* the growth rate of the whole capital stock rises, there are two forces at work on the growth of circulating capital and they are pulling in opposite directions. It is perfectly possible, if there is a strong switch to fixed capital, that the growth rate of the whole capital stock may rise, while that of the circulating capital component actually falls. The expansion of the demand for labour may thus be slowed up by the 'inventions', which have indeed been 'labour-saving', not only with respect to the labour most immediately affected, but over the economy as a whole.[1]

It is not at all unreasonable to suppose that something of this kind did indeed happen in England, during the first

[1] We are used to learning from Keynes that a tendency for an expansion of investment relatively to saving makes for an expansion in employment; so an argument which appears to run the other way is bound to be suspect. It should however be noticed that it is the same argument as has passed into orthodoxy in England (especially since the advent of Mr. Wilson's government). Productivity per man, we are told, is rising—it must rise if industry is to be kept competitive. But a rise in productivity will lead to unemployment, unless it expresses itself in a rise in total output. A growth of output needs working (circulating) capital to support it; hence it requires saving (private or public).

The truth is, we should now be able to understand, that sometimes (and for some purposes) the one kind of argument is right, sometimes the other. Keynes had in mind a depressed economy. One of the symptoms of depression is an abundance of stocks, at many stages of the productive process—stocks which cannot be used, because the will (or the incentive) to use them is lacking. The link between circulating capital and the demand for labour is therefore broken. This however is a special condition; ordinarily there is a link. There is a link even in the short run, at the top of a boom, in 'Full Employment'. And in the long run there is always a link. Sometimes it is looser, sometimes tighter; but on the average, over a period of years, it must be there.

It may nevertheless be asked just how it would show itself, in the early nineteenth-century conditions of which I am writing. Employment would rise, while credit expanded; why do we suppose that the expansion comes to a stop? There are two cases. If foreign trade is impeded, as in the later days of the war, the point would be reached at which further expansion would mean a fall in real wages; that certainly happened, but it is not our question; we are asking what expansion

quarter, or even the first third, of the nineteenth century—
though doubtless there were other complications (such as
reactions on foreign trade, and the obstacles to foreign trade
imposed by the war with Napoleon) not here taken into
account. Even a moderate swing in this direction, coupled
with the fact of increasing population, would be sufficient to
explain the general absence of labour shortage and the conse-
quent failure of real wages to rise (or to rise at all considerably). It was nevertheless to be expected (as Ricardo did in
fact expect) that the time would come when the adverse
effect of the swing to fixed capital would be exhausted, so that
the favourable effect of the higher growth rate would alone
survive.

'I have before observed' (he says)[1] 'that the increase in net incomes,[2]
estimated in commodities, which is always the consequence of improved
machinery, will lead to new savings and accumulations. These savings,
it must be remembered, are annual and must soon create a fund much
greater than the gross revenue originally lost by the discovery of the
machine, when the demand for labour will be as great as before, and the
situation of the people will be still further improved by the increased
savings which the increased net revenue will still enable them to make.'

This is valid, when correctly understood; but it is not quite
the whole story. Ricardo is assuming that there is just a single
switch to fixed capital; but why? Why should it not continue?
There is a reason, which he did not give, but which should be
added. As we have seen, the impulse to the introduction of the
new fixed capital, or 'machinery', was the reduction in the
costs of producing it; as a result of that reduction, it became
advantageous to use mechanical methods instead of the
handicraft methods previously employed. But this cheapening
was not once for all; it went on. One of the results of that would
indeed be the application of mechanical methods to new uses,

could occur without real wages falling. In peace-time (gold standard) conditions
as after 1819, the strain would be felt by the Bank of England through an adverse
movement of the balance of payments. If the gold standard had been suspended,
there would have been reversion, sooner or later, to the first case.

[1] Ricardo, *Principles*, p. 396 of vol. I of the Sraffa edition (Cambridge 1951).

[2] In the terminology Ricardo is here using, *net income* (or *net revenue*) means
profits+rents; *gross revenue* means *net revenue*+wages. (See his Chapter 26 on
'Gross and Net Revenue'.)

a continuation of what had happened in the first round. But another would be the replacement of the first generation of fixed capital goods (now relatively expensive and inefficient) by a new generation that was cheaper and more efficient; this would further increase profits (or 'net revenue' in Ricardo's terminology) *without any additional saving being required*. Once the initial fixed capital stock has been accumulated (and we shall now be under no temptation to minimize the pain and grief involved in that initial accumulation), it will itself, by further technical progress, gain in productive power; this later growth imposes no strain upon savings, so that it has a purely favourable effect upon the demand for labour. This is the point—we shall now be able to understand why it took so long to reach it—when the surplus of labour can be absorbed, and real wages can begin decisively to rise.[1]

This, I believe, is the root of the matter; it is the main thing which has to be said, so long as we are content to concern ourselves, in what would nowadays be called a 'macroeconomic' manner, with the *general level* of wages. But as soon as we look, even a little, beyond that, there is another change in the labour market, of quite decisive importance, which must be added.

Though labour was on the point of acquiring its 'class-consciousness', different sections of what was soon to regard itself as the working class were affected in different ways. A

[1] I have taken much advantage, in this summary of the 'macro-economic' argument, of the constancy of the level of real wages, which for my particular purpose could, I think, be properly assumed. (It was this which enabled me to follow Ricardo so closely). Fixed capital, like circulating capital, was supposed to be valued in terms of the wage-cost of the labour embodied; so long as real wages are taken as constant, this comes to the same thing as valuing it in terms of the consumption-good price-level (taking a suitable unit). The value of the capital stock (the whole capital stock) is then an unambiguous concept; and the equation of saving (measured in terms of consumption goods given up) to investment (the increment in the value of the capital stock) presents no difficulty. It is quite a different matter when we come to the stage when real wages rise. The analysis which then becomes necessary baffled the economists of the late nineteenth century; it is only in our time beginning to become clear. It was fortunately unnecessary for my purpose to enter upon that difficult territory.

new industrial working class was coming into existence, which was different from the old *urban proletariat*—one of the main differences being that it was more *regularly* employed.

When one thinks of the fluctuations to which industry is subject, and has always been subject, this may seem to be a paradoxical statement; none the less it is true. The industrial worker was subject to unemployment; but when he was employed, he was regularly employed. He was not a casual worker, who never even thought he knew how he would be employed in a few weeks' time. It was casual labour that was the typical condition of the pre-industrial proletariat; the state of industrial labour was different. The long hours and miserable conditions of the early industrial worker are familiar; but there was this gain that went with them, which in the long run would be a decisive gain, the gain in regularity.

Modern industry was bound to move in the direction of regularity, just because of the characteristic on which I have been insisting, its dependence upon the use of fixed capital. It could only be profitable to produce in the new way if the durable equipment could be kept in use. If it was to be kept in use, it must have a more or less permanent organization, with a more or less permanent labour force attached, to operate it. This had consequences of the first importance, both social and economic.

The pre-industrial proletariat had been rootless, but the industrial worker was not rootless; he was a member of a group. It was a group that would soon be demanding a place in wider society; but even before that, its formation had deep effects upon the lives of those who composed it. The protection from association with one's fellows, which had been present to some extent (as we have seen) in the old-style village, had come back again in a new form.[1] Thus it was

[1] It is tempting to associate this social change with the change in population behaviour which seems to have accompanied it. If that could be verified, it would enable us to explain the population movement as part of the general change which we have been analysing, instead of bringing it in from outside, as I have been doing. But this is only a guess; the causes of the upsurge of population in England, that began some time in the late eighteenth century, are still very much of a mystery.

that the industrial worker was able to organize; he could do so, because he found himself in a situation in which the elements of organization were already present. Even without formal organization, he had a little more security from the industrial system itself. Only a little more, since he was exposed to personal injustice and to the effects of business upheavals; but enough to feel the shock of its deprivation when it failed, and to attempt, by combination with his fellows, to make it go further. He would then discover that he was in a position to exercise a bargaining power that had previously been lacking. The groups he had formed were essential to employers; he could therefore use the strike weapon, that was formerly unavailable. It is obvious that Trade Unions, and even Labour Parties, are among the consequences of industrialism; this is the reason why.

So what was missing from our previous 'macro-economic' analysis was that it neglected the way in which industrial workers (in the wide sense of workers in the new trades that had grown up with industrialism) were enabled to make themselves, first in small groups, and gradually in wider groups, into a class that was somewhat better privileged than the casual workers who still remained outside. Thus their wages would rise, well before the point was reached when the general surplus of labour was removed. Then, as the surplus began to be removed, there could be spread of organization even among what was left of the casual workers—through General Workers' Unions, Trade Boards, and so on. Thus it appeared that it was organization that led to the higher wages; though that, in fact, was no more than a part of the truth.

I have so far been treating the impact of industrialism on the labour market in terms of British experience; but the experience which is relevant is not just British; it is worldwide. It is as a world phenomenon that we, in these days, most need to consider it. In Britain, the absorption of the proletariat into an industrial working class is substantially completed; and in most other 'advanced' countries it is very nearly complete. But in the world as a whole it is not complete; and it often seems that it is not even making progress.

Partly, of course, (as before) this is a matter of population pressure. Whatever may be the reason for the upsurge in population that began in Europe a century and more ago, that for the 'population explosion' of our time is well understood. Malthus was right in holding that human population will increase quite rapidly, unless there is something to check it; one of the most powerful of the checks which operated in the past has been, in many countries, rather suddenly removed. Science has found it easy, and cheap, to suppress (or almost to suppress) some of the most destructive and debilitating diseases;[1] population has responded, as Malthus would have expected that it would. Nor has this increasing population been checked, in the other manner foreshadowed by Malthus, by pressure on the food supply; for science has come to the rescue there too. There has been such an increase in agricultural output, over the world as a whole, that (save in particular places and for particular reasons—and then on no greater scale than was usual in the past) there has been no famine. But the increase in agricultural output has not been attended by a proportional increase in agricultural workers; the movement, at least so far, has been away from the land, not towards it.[2] In spite of that, the supply of food, in general throughout the world, has not failed to meet the need. The failure has been in the absorption of the growing population, which remains, in great part, a proletariat—a pre-industrial proletariat.

As before, it is chiefly in the cities that one finds it. But not in London, or Paris, or Birmingham, the places where one would have found it in the nineteenth century. It is in the cities of the underdeveloped world, of Latin America and of Africa, in Bombay and Calcutta and Djakarta, and (surely

[1] The strongest case is the eradication, or near-eradication, of malaria from many previously infected areas. For a very convincing demonstration of the effect of this on the population movement—some of it working quite indirectly—see P. K. Newman, Malaria eradication and population growth (Michigan University School of Public Health 1965).

[2] See above, p. 120.

also) in Canton and Shanghai.[1] And now it is not only for the old reason—that some are thought to be making fortunes, or just to be 'making good'—that a surplus of labour is being drawn into the cities; that 'demonstration effect' has been reinforced by others. Education, which makes people expect jobs, jobs of the new kind; the propaganda of politicians, and of economists, which has promoted economic growth to be a human right; the installation of new national governments, looked on as job-providing agencies; these are the charmers who are swelling the crowds, who now wait at the gates to be brought in. Why, they ask (or it is asked for them), cannot the transformation which was accomplished in the advanced countries in the nineteenth and early twentieth century be repeated for them? The expansion that is needed, in order that these millions should be absorbed, is indeed enormous; but the expansive power of Modern Industry—the fully science-based industry of the twentieth century—is also enormous. Is it impossible that it could cope?

After all, enormous though the task may appear, it is not really so out of scale. When we look at the matter in world terms, and consider what has been done, it looks far from impossible. Two hundred years ago the industrial working class was hardly in existence, anywhere; 100 years ago it can have numbered no more than quite a few millions; today it is vastly larger. In order to calculate the total number of those who are now 'inside', we should add to the manufacturing populations of the advanced countries the 'white-collar' workers who are their necessary helpers, together with the farmers whose productive activities have been transformed by industrialization; we should take all these (including their

---

[1] For this is not a disease that can be cured by organizational change, by the substitution of one government for another. The most that can be done by a powerful government is to do as the Russians have done, to restrict the formation of an *urban* proletariat by controlling the movement of labour, keeping labour on the land until a place is ready for it. (This has been possible for them, largely because of their inheritance of an administrative machine that was built up in the days of serfdom; and which, even after serfdom was formally abolished in 1861, retained many marks of its origin.)

Such a 'solution' can hardly have been open to the communists of China, who inherited from their predecessors a vast urban proletariat already formed.

families) and not forget to include the by no means negligible number of those who are in corresponding sectors of the less developed countries; it is outside all these that the line should be drawn. No exact, or nearly exact, figure for their total could possibly be given; but it is quite safe to say that it could not be less than 500 millions. That is less than the population of China alone, about the same as the population of India, probably something less than one-sixth of the population of the world. The number to be absorbed is therefore vast; but the number that has been absorbed is also very large. The rate of expansion that is needed to absorb the remainder—if we allow a couple of generations in which to do it (and no one could seriously expect that it could be achieved in less)— is certainly no greater than that which has been achieved hitherto. Further population increase will indeed make it more difficult; but even so, when the task is measured in this way, it does not look impossible.

> God hath wrought things as incredible
> For his people of old; what hinders now?

says the Chorus in *Samson*.

I am afraid there are hindrances.

X

CONCLUSION

IT would be absurd, and out of proportion, to embark in a concluding chapter on any serious discussion of the Modern Phase, which is the state the world is in at the present day. All I shall do (for it is a responsibility I can hardly escape) is to state my own opinion on the great question that was raised at the end of the preceding chapter.

I believe that it is, in rather a deep sense, a political question. If there were no nations—if everyone could go where he liked, was just as acceptable wherever he went, and was willing to go wherever he was wanted—the Absorption of the whole human race into the ranks of the developed would be relatively simple. Even so, it would take time; and it may well be that even in the century, or century and a half, that may be held to have elapsed since the beginning of the process we were considering, not enough time has been allowed. We have seen that until the Absorption was completed, or within sight of completion, there would—on this assumption—be no general rise in real wages; so, even to the liberal and to the internationally minded, it is perhaps not so very agreeable an assumption after all.

It is, in any case, not an assumption that we are entitled to make; and I, for my part, would not want to make it. The attachment to one's own people, and to the dwelling-place of one's own people, has far too much that is good and lovely about it for one to wish it to disappear. The groups that have formed nations, and some of the groups within nations, are social units that have value; by putting them into a 'melting pot' much is lost. When we examine our aspiration, it is for a

Development, an Absorption, which is consistent with the maintenance of social identity.

Even that, though economically more difficult, is in principle by no means unattainable. There was a time when a movement towards it seemed (much more clearly than it does now) to be dominant; in the nineteenth century, in the era of (more or less) Free Trade. What we might expect to have happened, if that movement had continued without interruption, was a gradual increase in the *number* of developed countries, and a consequential gradual decrease in the number of those who still remained behind, or 'outside'. It would have been no more than a gradual movement—not fast enough, it may well be, to satisfy the expectations which it would have aroused; and it would have been subject to fluctuations, general fluctuations and fluctuations affecting particular countries, which would have meant that every now and then the general direction would have seemed to be lost. Nevertheless, if we grant the continued advancement of science, and the accumulation of capital which would follow, if it were not prevented, the process should have continued and should have gone through.

But notice what it implies. Though the formerly developed countries would not be made absolutely poorer by the spread of development, their relative position would have been damaged. England, at the beginning, was the 'workshop of the world'; after the United States and Germany had come up, England was no more than a single industrialized country, like others. When, as must surely have happened next (apart from political events), Russia and Japan were the major new arrivals, it would have been the Germans and Americans who found themselves in a weaker—political—position. The expansion, or Absorption, could not take place, in a world of nation states, without political implications.

The regulation of trade, for *national* purposes, has a history that extends over many years; it goes back, at least, to the so-called 'mercantilism' of the seventeenth and eighteenth centuries.[1] 'Mercantilism' marks the discovery that economic

---

[1] I have deliberately avoided using the term 'mercantilism' in this book, until

growth can be used *in the national interest*; as a means to national objectives of all sorts, including the pursuit of influence over other nations, of prestige and of power. These are objectives, we must allow, which no government that is concerned with the maintenance of its own independence can entirely overlook. Yet this first mercantilism was a failure; and was succeeded, for a while, by the era of Free Trade.

There were many reasons for that—ideological reasons, internal political pressures and so on; they are familiar enough, and I shall not enter into them. It was quite as important, I believe, that the old mercantilism was an administrative failure; its proponents did not have the administration (or, for that matter, the economics) which were needed to see it through. When these things became available, the situation changed.

The Administrative Revolution in Government (as I have been calling it) is a change—unlike most of the transformations with which I have been concerned—that can (almost) be precisely dated. Its crucial date is that of the First World War (1914–18). Before the war, there had been developments that had foreshadowed it; the Limited Liability Company and the beginnings of Central Banking are among the most significant. But it was during the war that governments discovered—to their astonishment and sometimes to their dismay—what power, what economic power, what power over their own peoples had come into their hands. Some, when the war was over, endeavoured to forget it; only to be driven to resurrecting it, bit by bit, as the easiest way of coping with one after another of the emergencies, political and economic, which they encountered. Others, such as the explicitly Revolutionary governments of Russia, and later China, coming into power in countries where the Mercantile Economy had

this late stage. This was because I wanted to make my main theme the growth of the Mercantile Economy, not neglecting its relations with the State, but keeping that, as it were, 'outside'. The name 'mercantilist' is only appropriate when we are looking at history the other way, from the standpoint of the State, from the standpoint of the rulers. They become 'mercantilist' when they begin to realize that the merchants can be used as an instrument for their primarily non-mercantile purposes.

not penetrated deeply, seized with avidity upon the opportunity which it presented to them. It was their doctrines which were responsible for their attitude towards it; but their ability to put their doctrines into practice depended on the Administrative Revolution which had there as elsewhere occurred. It was through the Administrative Revolution that they were enabled to recreate their classical bureaucracies in a modern form.

The new techniques, and the institutions that embodied them, could be used in various ways and for various objectives. They could be used in a new way, for the attainment of social objectives—'welfare'—that had formerly been quite out of reach. But they could also be used in the old way: for the regulation of trade, and economic activity generally, *in the national interest*.

In the days before the Administrative Revolution, the weapons that were available to governments for the execution of a policy of economic nationalism were primitive. Tariffs became established as the principal form of protection, because they were the principal instrument which at that stage was usable. But far less could be done by simple import tariffs than by the more sophisticated means that were now at the governments' disposal. Quantitative controls, import and export monopolies, controls over capital movements (outgoing and incoming), manipulations of the tax system (even such as appear on the surface to be internal taxes); new devices, that go the same way, are continually invented. The most thoroughgoing of all is the bringing of those who make the decisions about trade and investment under the direct control of government. Communism itself, in one of its aspects, is the extreme—the ultimate—form of protection.

It is curious, at first sight, that it is not the advanced countries, but the others, who (on the whole) have carried their protectionism furthest. For it is the 'underdeveloped world', taken as a whole, which in consequence of these tendencies suffers most. One can nevertheless understand why it happens.

One of the vehicles of mercantile expansion, in the Free

Trade era, was colonialism; from what was said about colonization in an earlier chapter,[1] that would be expected. Colonialism, when it went so far as the direct imposition of an alien rule, was an outrage on national sentiment; even when it did not go so far, contenting itself with 'concessions' and extra-territorialities, the example of what had happened elsewhere aroused a fear that corresponded. The governments that were imposed upon the dependencies might be conducted on liberal principles; but that meant that they gave scope for opposition to themselves to build up. The governments that have succeeded them, being based upon a nationalism that had become articulate in opposition, are understandably nationalistic. They are hostile, on principle, to international capital. They insist on attempting to develop themselves from their own exiguous resources, supplemented (it may be) by more or less politically motivated 'aid'. This is not the spreading, and is much less effective than the spreading, which on the other plan should have occurred.[2]

Yet, strong as these political forces are, I am not suggesting that they are the only explanation. There is an economic reason which, in the light of what was said in the last chapter about the beginnings of industrialism, we should be able to see in perspective.

Remember Ricardo on 'machinery'. An improvement, he showed, was very liable at a first round to be labour-saving; but the accumulation of capital, out of the extra profits which were made in these early stages, should subsequently lead to an increase in the demand for labour. If one is confining one's attention to a single country in which labour (at least

[1] Above, pp. 49–54.
[2] The case of Russia itself is not fundamentally dissimilar. The Russians' hostility to capital was (at the least) aggravated by the fact that the chief capital which they knew was foreign capital. They have made a much better hand at autarkic development than the majority of underdeveloped countries have done, or are likely to do, chiefly because of the greater variety of natural resources that are at their disposal. Yet they have not been able to avoid going through the pain and grief, which is characteristic of the early stage of an Industrial Revolution, when adequate capital cannot be drawn from abroad. Those less fortunately situated could not achieve the same result, under that restriction, even at a comparable cost.

in the end) is fairly mobile from one occupation to another, that makes sense, and agrees with experience; the labour that is thrown out will be re-absorbed, and as a shortage of labour appears, wages will rise. But in the international economy, even such as was created for a while by the dominance of Free Trade, though there is the same sequence, its implication is different. For the labour that is thrown out may be in one country, and the expansion in demand for labour, which is the effect of the accumulation of capital that results, may be in another. The English handloom weavers, who were displaced by textile machinery, could (in the end and after much travail) find re-employment in England; but what of the Indian weavers who were displaced by the same improvement? Even in their case there would be a favourable effect, somewhere; but it might be anywhere; there would be no particular reason why it should be in India. The poorer the country, the narrower will be its range of opportunities; the more likely, therefore, it is that it will suffer long-lasting damage, now and then, from a backwash of improvements that have occurred elsewhere.

Even in already industrialized countries, mobility of labour is not perfect; so that they also, though to a lesser degree and more obviously temporarily, have their backward areas and their depressed industries. It is, also for them, a motive for protectionism. But one can understand that in the poorer countries there is an even greater desire to protect themselves from this sort of damage. It is damage which in some cases they have actually suffered; more often, it is damage that has not yet been suffered, but is feared. It is difficult to blame them; it must nevertheless be recognized (and is increasingly being recognized) that the high-cost industries that are set up behind these shields do not engender the profit—to the national economy as a whole—which would serve as a basis for further growth. Something can be done, by these methods, in the way of alleviation; but the expansion they permit is strictly limited.

Whatever its motives, protectionism is an obstacle; but the protectionism that arises from the motives so far examined need not be an insuperable obstacle. As the epoch of colonialism recedes, its memory may fade; forms of international investment less wounding to national pride can be, and have been, discovered. It is beginning to be recognized, on the other side, that to keep a socially unprofitable industry in permanent existence by protecting it is foolish. Temporary use of such measures for the easing of transitions is defensible; their permanent use is not. Commercial agreements, though the forms that they take are often so impregnated with nationalism, can facilitate trade, and can therefore make openings for expansion internationally.

So it is possible, perhaps probable, that along these roads the path may be cleared. Yet even so there remains a further danger. One must not allow oneself to be unduly influenced by the events of a single decade; recent experience is nevertheless suggestive; it seems (most uncomfortably) to fit in.

Though the Administrative Revolution has strengthened Government in so many respects, there are others in which its effect has been the reverse. When it is known that governments have these powers, it is harder for them to say 'no'— to social expenditure, to prestige expenditure, or to any expenditure for which support can be whipped up. Economists have taught them how to do their accounts so as to accommodate these things; far more has been accommodated (very much, in many ways, to the general advantage) than in earlier times would have been thought to be at all possible. But economic administrators, however ingenious, cannot stretch resources indefinitely. The point must be reached when there is a strain.

The symptoms of the strain are familiar: inflation, balance-of-payments deficits, a variety of monetary and exchange disorders. But these are no more than symptoms; the cause lies deeper. The symptoms will not be removed—they will only change their forms—by technical adjustments: purely monetary arrangements, changes in monetary policy. So long as the resources, of the richer countries, are kept under strain, what they have to spare for furthering the growth of the *world* economy, is bound to be restricted. Not much will happen from clearing the ditches in the fields if the river, that might have irrigated the fields, is diverted.

That will have to do. I think it will be agreed that I have covered, as promised, a vast field; I do not need to apologize for the fact, especially obvious towards the end, that much of it, has been covered very superficially. I am very prepared to believe that many of the examples I have chosen would not stand up to closer examination. I would, however, recall the *statistical* principle with which I began. On that principle, I should not be much disturbed if in a particular instance the reason for a change turned out to be different from that which I alleged. A particular bank, for instance, may have come up in a different way from that which I sketched, but that does not matter; my business has been with the general way in which banks (and all the rest) have come up. So interpreted, I am hopeful that what I have been saying makes some sense.

I said at the beginning that I should not be giving *economic history* a narrow interpretation. I hope that I have carried out that promise. I have tried to exhibit economic history, in the way that the great eighteenth-century writers did, as part of a social evolution much more widely considered. I have tried to indicate the lines that connect the economic story with the things we ordinarily regard as falling outside it. But when one becomes conscious of these links, one realizes that recognition is not enough. There are threads that run from economics into other social fields, into politics, into religion, into science and into technology; they develop there, and then run back into economics. These I have made little attempt to follow out; but I am in no way concerned to deny their existence.

APPENDIX

RICARDO ON MACHINERY

RICARDO was fond of arithmetical examples; but he did not work one out for his chapter on Machinery. This is probably one of the reasons why the important doctrine of that chapter has not received more attention. I have made much use of it in what I have said on the Industrial Revolution. It may be helpful if I try to construct an example myself.

Let us begin (to make things a little easier) with a stationary economy; but let us suppose that 'machines' of a sort are already being used. One such machine (or complex of machines) takes one year to make, and lasts for ten years. It takes ten labour-units to make it, and ten to operate it in each of the ten years of its life. It will then produce, each year, 100 units of *product*—to be thought of as a 'consumption goods bundle'. We are concerned with the demand for labour at a fixed rate of real wages, so we can keep the wage of a labour-unit fixed in terms of the *product*. Suppose that it is 8 units of *product*.

With these figures, there will be a *surplus* of *product* over wages. This is most simply regarded as *consumption out of profits*. It should nevertheless be remembered, if we allow ourselves to use that description, that the *consumption out of profits* may be public as well as private (in a socialist economy, to which the argument applies, it could all be public). And it should also be remembered that if some part of the wage is saved, or taken in taxes, *consumption out of profits* (private and public) may be larger than the surplus with which we are concerned— the surplus of production over wages.

The 'social accounts' of our initially stationary economy

could be set out in the following form (taking the initial stock of machines to be 100):

	Employment of labour	Wage-bill	Output of product
Operating	1000	8000	10,000
Constructing	100	800	—
Total	1100	8800	
Surplus			1200

	Initial stock	Added	Discarded	Final stock
Machines	100	10	10	100

With these figures, the gross rate of profit on a single machine (profit before depreciation) is $(100-80)/80$; that is to say, it is 25 per cent per year.

Now suppose that a new machine is introduced, which takes the same time to construct, lasts the same time, and produces the same annual product; but instead of 10 labour-units, 15 are required to build it, while the number of labour-units required to operate it is reduced from 10 to 8. The gross rate of profit on the new machine, at the same rate of wages, is $(100-64)/120$, which is 30 per cent. Since the time-structure of the performance is the same, the net rate of return will be raised correspondingly. In pursuit of profit (or even of efficiency) there should therefore be a change to the new technique. Suppose there is. What happens?

Prospective profit has risen; so it is natural to expect that there will be a rise in consumption out of profits (however interpreted). Any such rise, as will appear in what follows, makes the adjustment more difficult. So it will be interesting to see what happens if there is no such rise. Let us therefore assume that the surplus of product over wages remains constant, at its original 1200 throughout.

In the first year that the new technique is introduced, there can be no significant change in the running account as set out above. The same old machines are still there, producing the same product and employing the same labour to operate them; the same 100 labour-units can still be employed in construction, consistently with a constant surplus. But the 100 labour-units will now be employed in constructing new machines. So the difference comes at the end of the year, when the final stock is 90 old machines (10 old machines, as before, having worn out) plus only 100/15 ($= 6 \cdot 67$) new machines.

So in the second year employment in operating is reduced to

$$90 \times 10 + 6 \cdot 67 \times 8 = 953 \text{ (approximately)}$$

and the output of *product* is reduced to

$$90 \times 100 + 6 \cdot 67 \times 100 = 9667$$

The accounts of the second year will thus come out as follows:

	Employment	Wage-bill	Product
Operating	953	7624	9667
Constructing	105	843	
Total	1058	8467	
Surplus			1200

Employment in constructing can only rise by 5 per cent if the surplus is to be kept the same.

For the machines in the second year, we shall then have

	Initial stock	Added	Discarded	Final stock
Old	90	—	10	80
New	6·67	7·0	—	13·67

Thus in the third year employment (and output) will contract still further, the very small increase in the number of new machines coming into operation being still far less than sufficient to balance the old machines that are wearing out.

It is unnecessary to write out the rest of the sequence in detail. The results which I get by turning the handle may be summarized as follows (with a little rounding). I reproduce

year 1, when employment and output are the same as in the previously existing stationary state.

Year	1	2	3	4	5	6
Employment	1100	1058	1021	989	969	952
Output of finished product	10000	9667	9367	9117	8917	8816

Year	7	8	9	10	11
Employment	949	962	996	1056	1150
Output	8800	8900	9166	9650	10400

I stop at the point at which the previous levels of output and employment of labour have been recovered.

We began from a stationary state, but at the end—the very long end—the economy is set upon a course of expansion. This is bound to be so, in the end, so long as any part of the additional profits are saved. A single improvement in technique, with suitable saving propensities (and no rise in wages) can convert a stationary into an expanding economy.

But the price, as we see, may be heavy. It could naturally be reduced by borrowing from abroad (if that were possible). It would also be reduced if it were possible to draw upon stocks of finished goods that had been previously accumulated. Temporary reductions in consumption, whether from profits or from wages, could also (in a sense) be an easement. These are the reasons why credit inflation (in Keynes's manner) can be an easement; though the problem with which we are here concerned is not Keynes's problem.

It should be noticed, in conclusion, that a principal reason for the violence of the effect, as it has appeared in this numerical example, is the high cost, in terms of labour, which I have attributed to the construction of the new machine. A reduction in that cost would have made things much easier. I have suggested in the text that this may have been a main way in which, in the historical case of the British Industrial Revolution, the alleviation came.

INDEX